DOROTHY AND THE WIZARD IN OZ

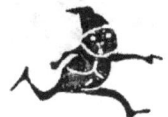

ILLUSTRATED BY

JOHN R. NEILL

—

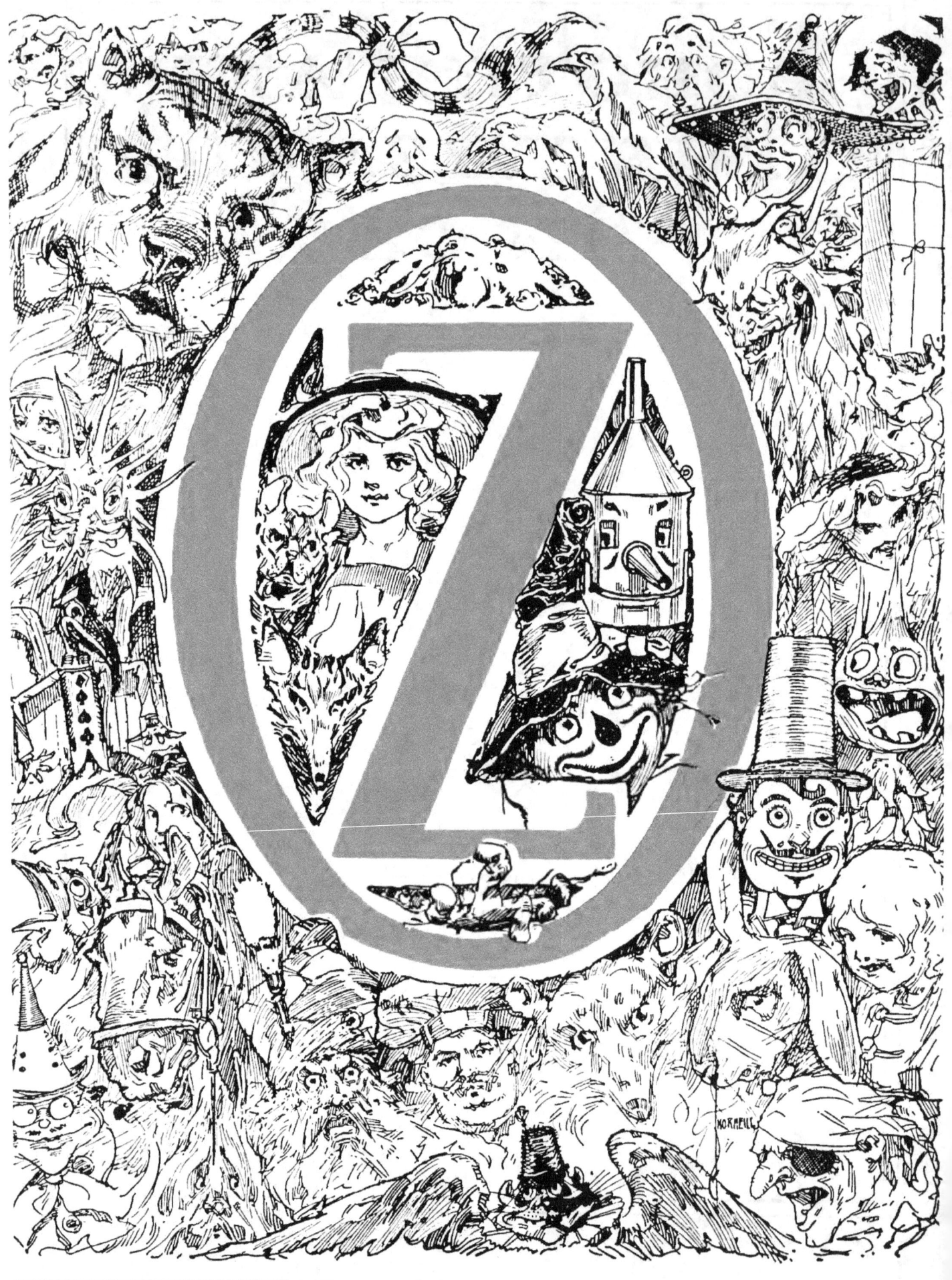

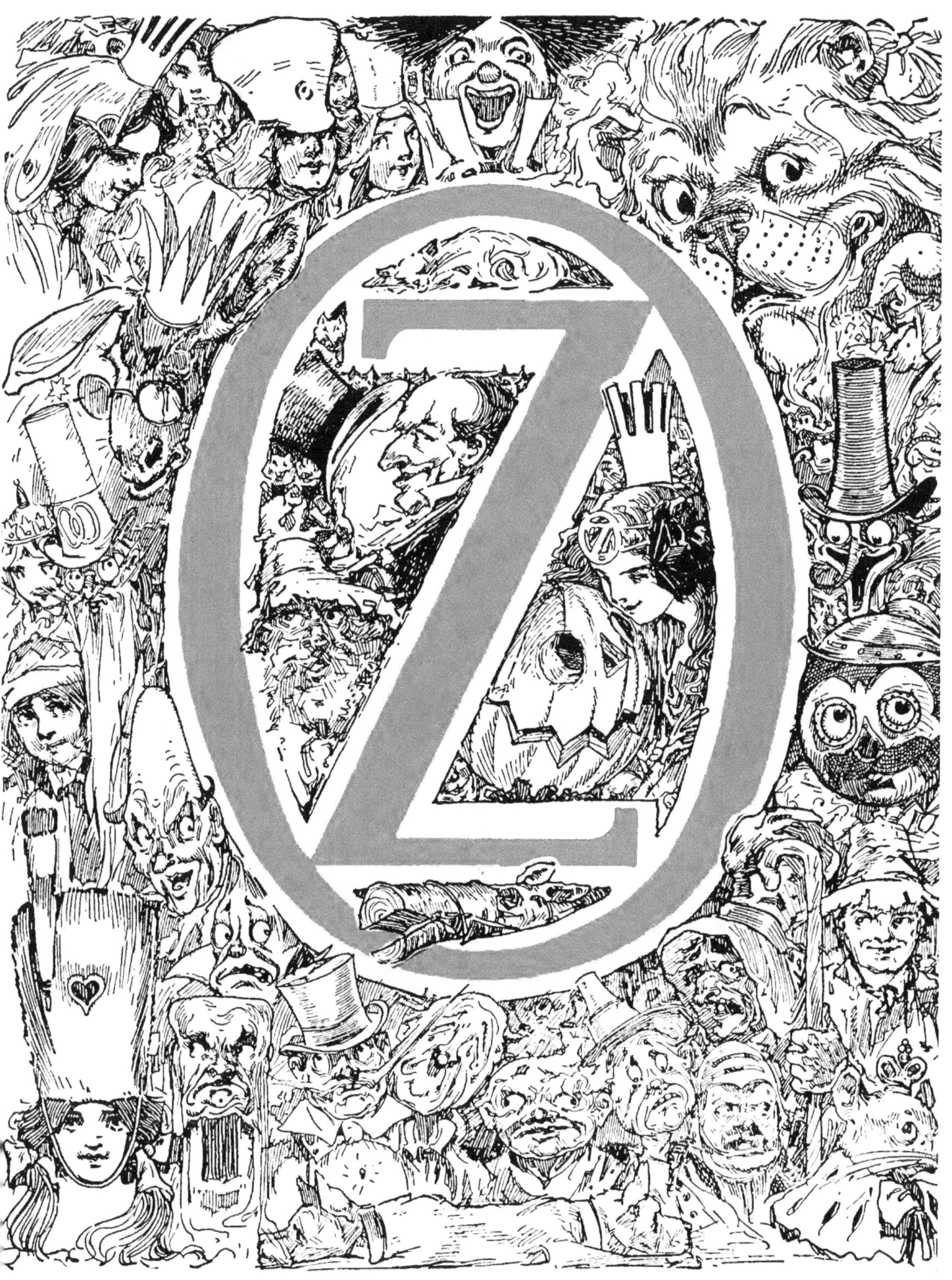

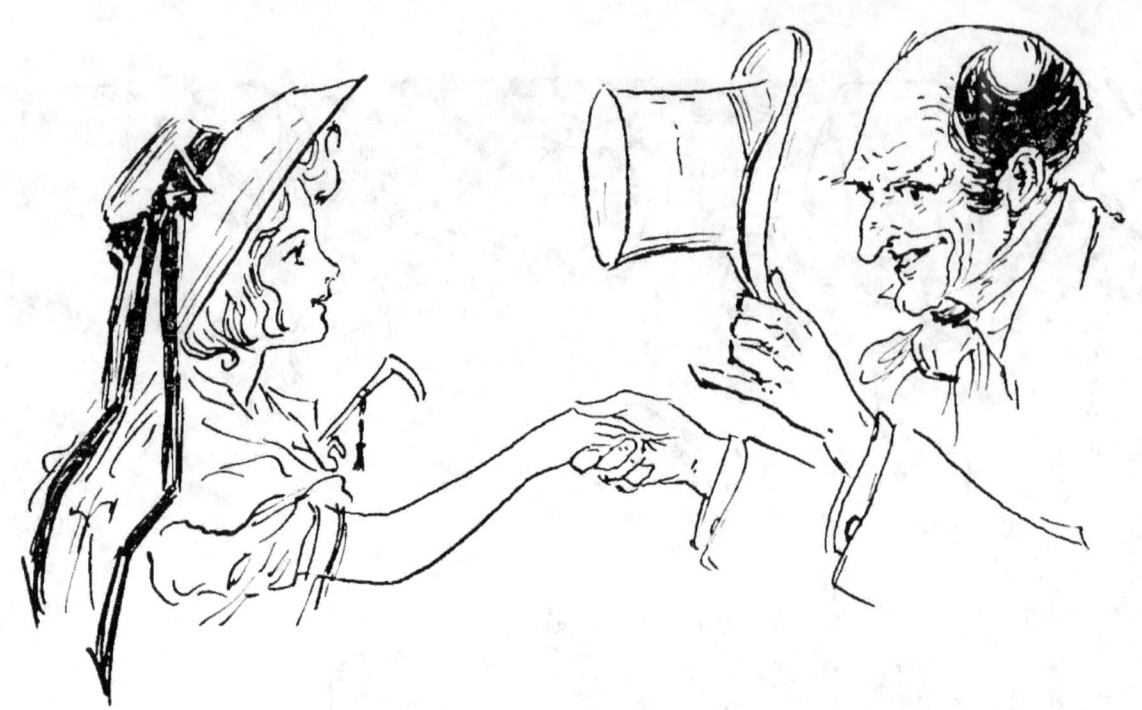

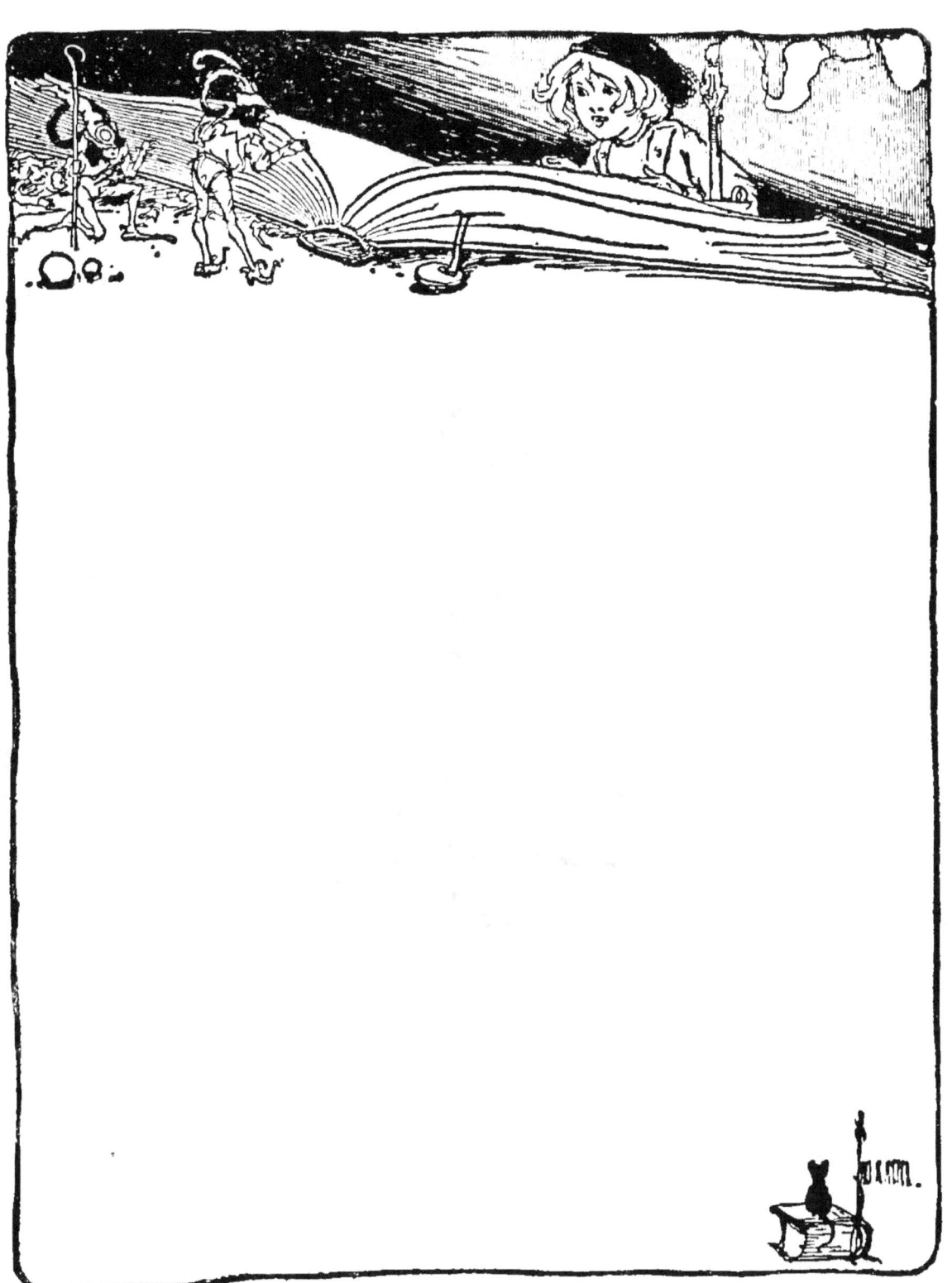

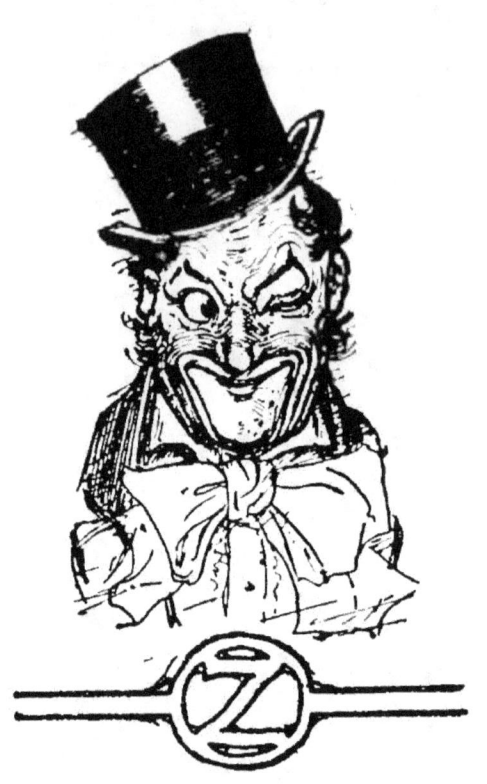

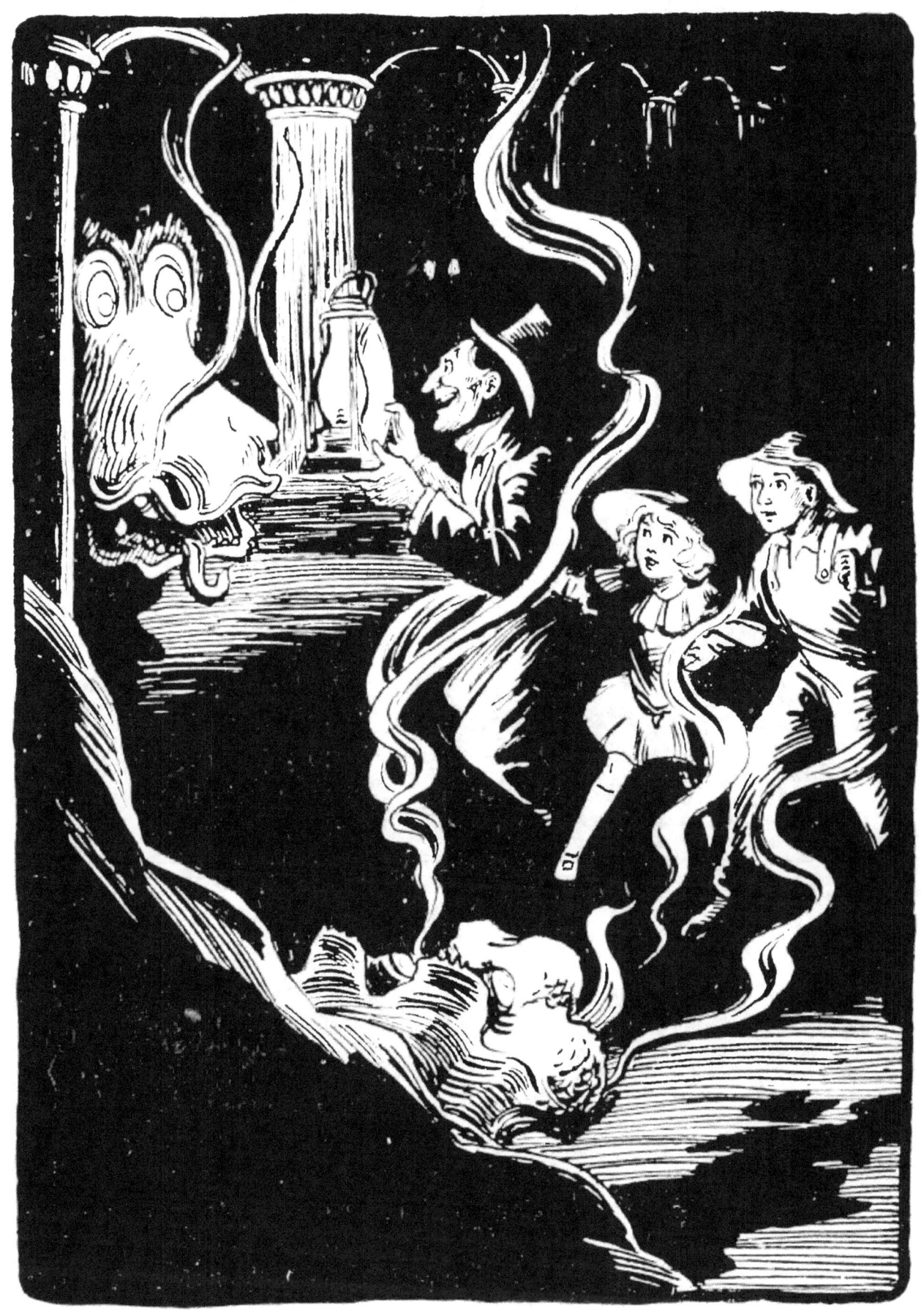

THE DEN OF THE DRAGONETTES

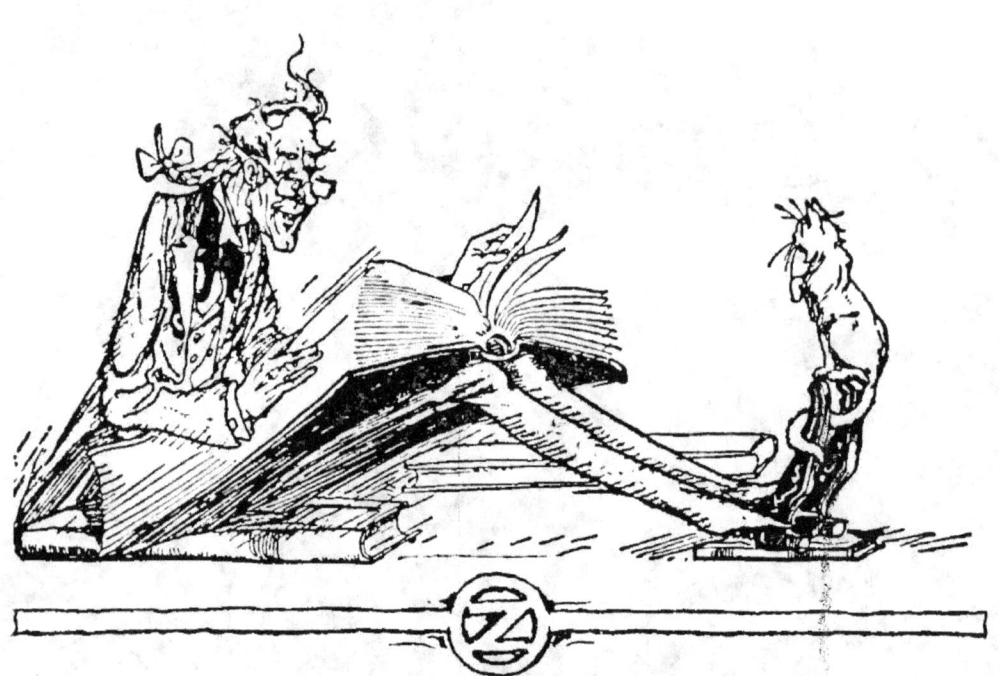

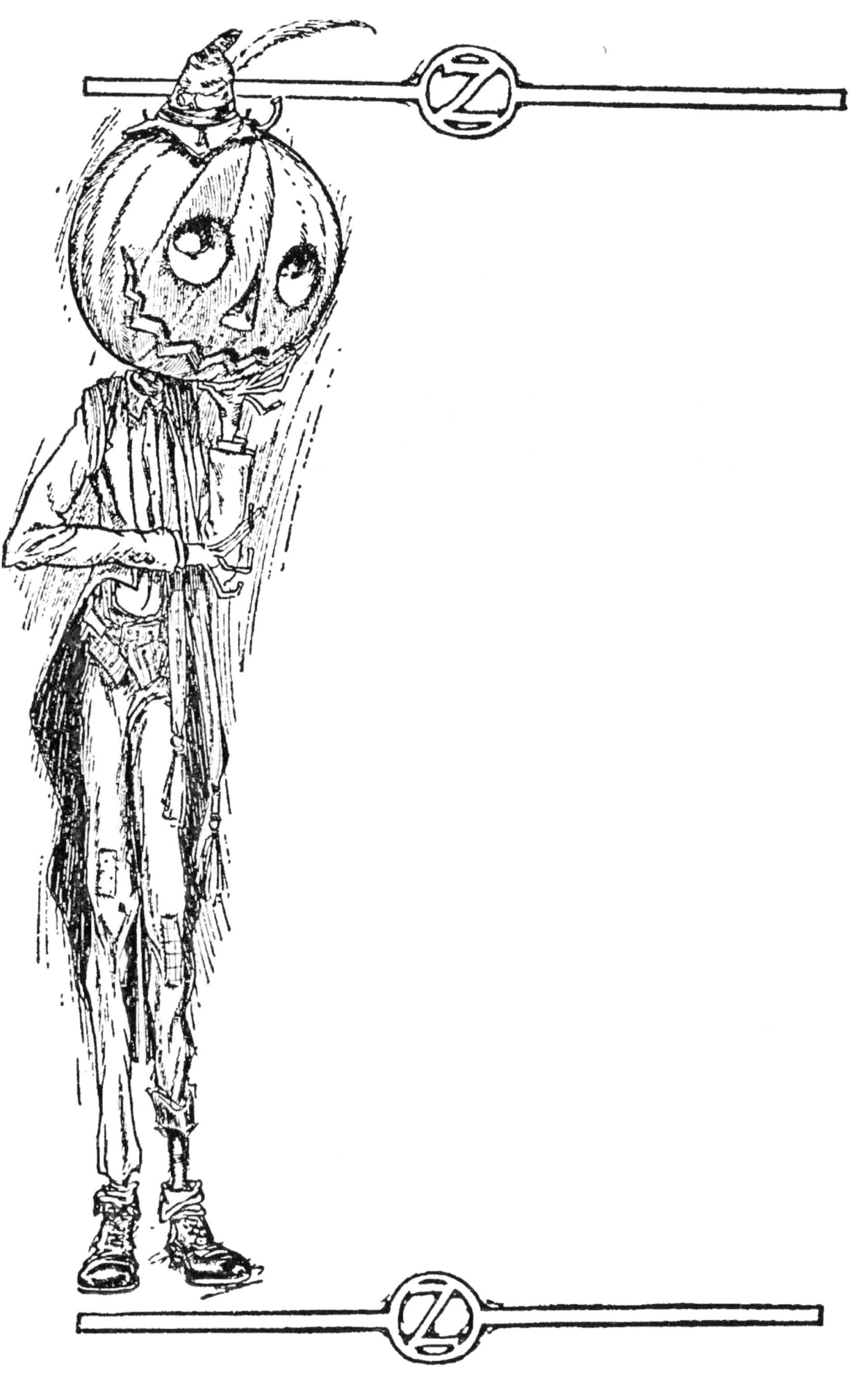

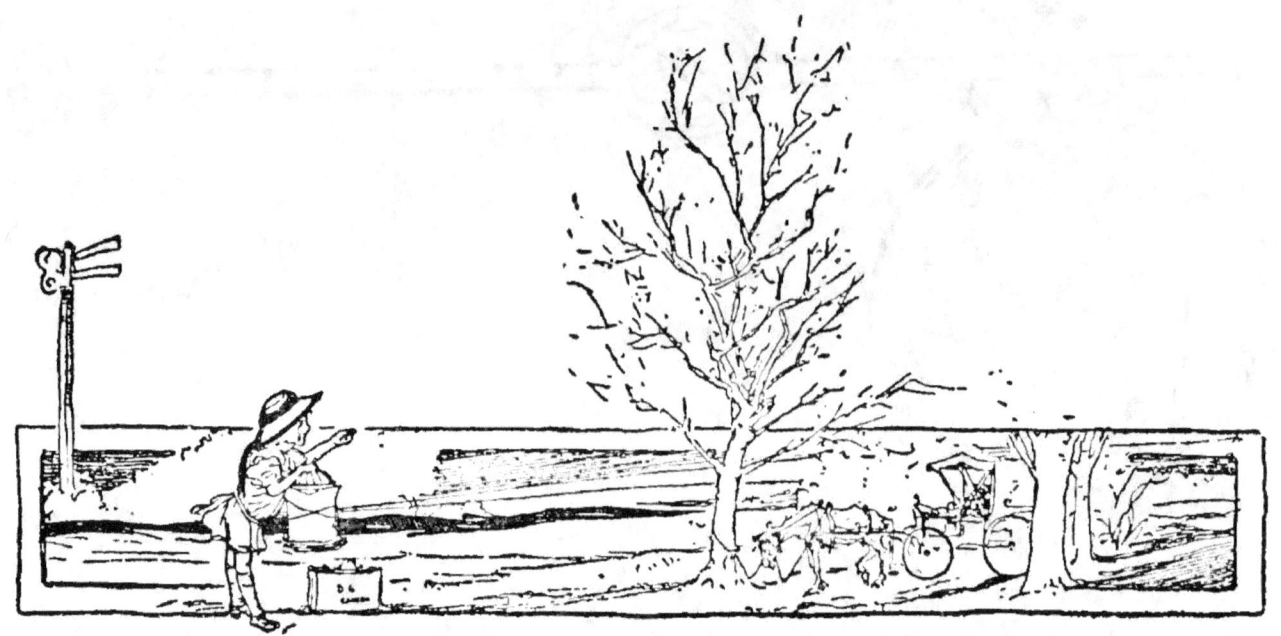

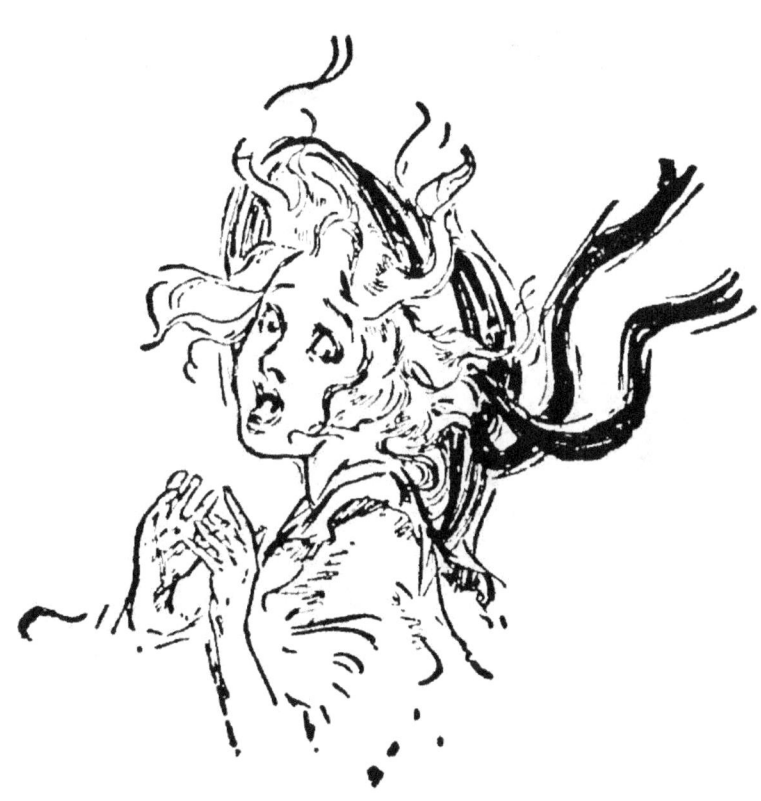

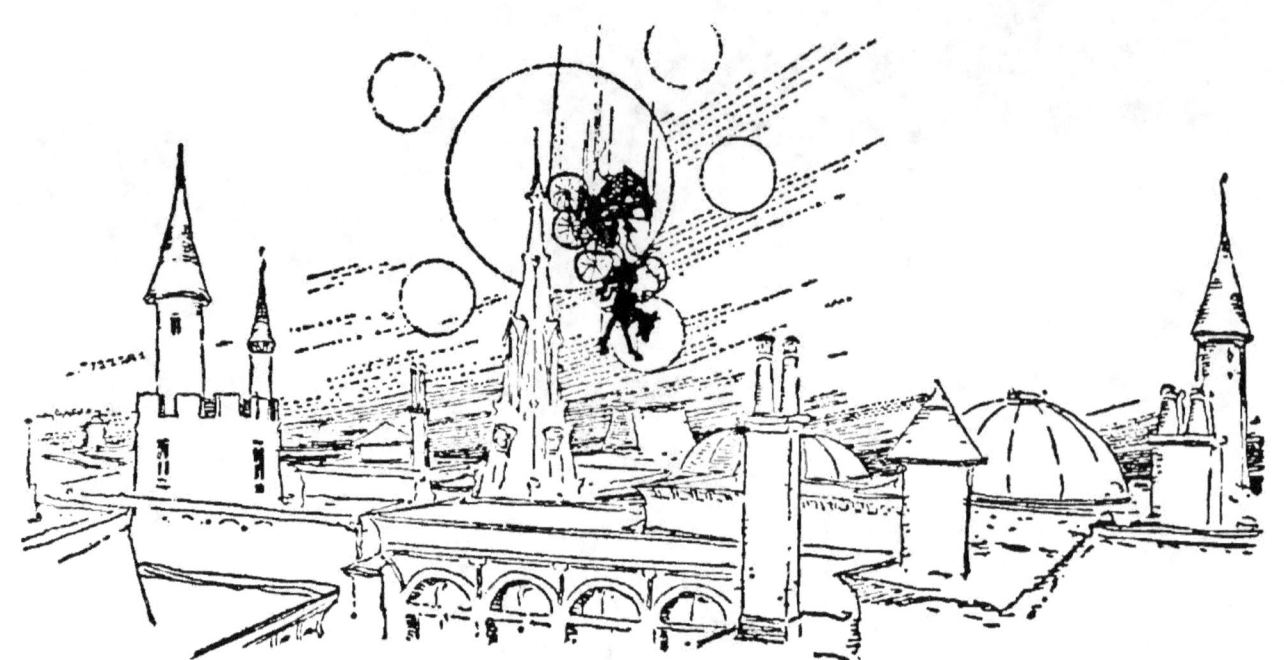

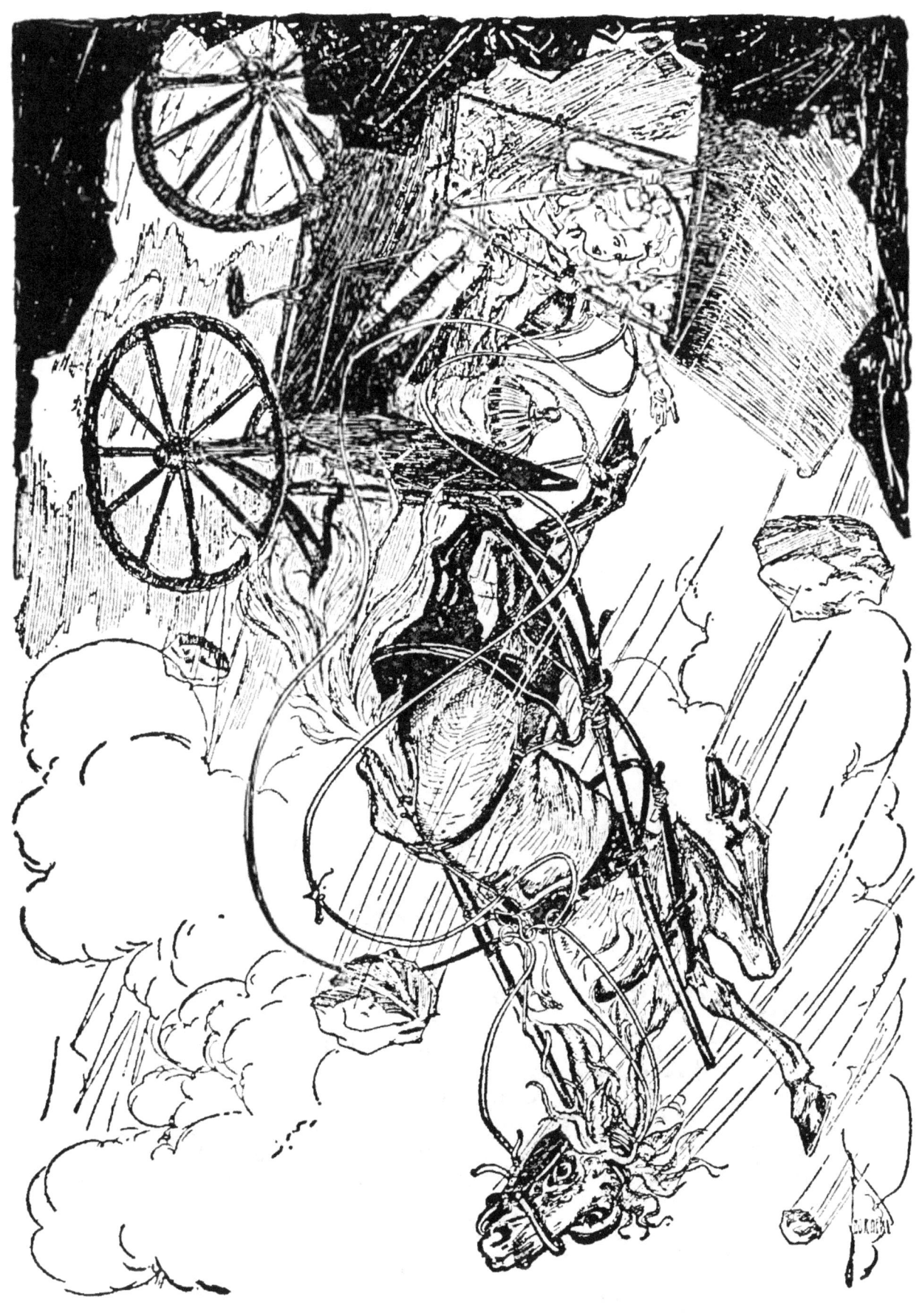

HORSE, BUGGY AND ALL FELL SLOWLY

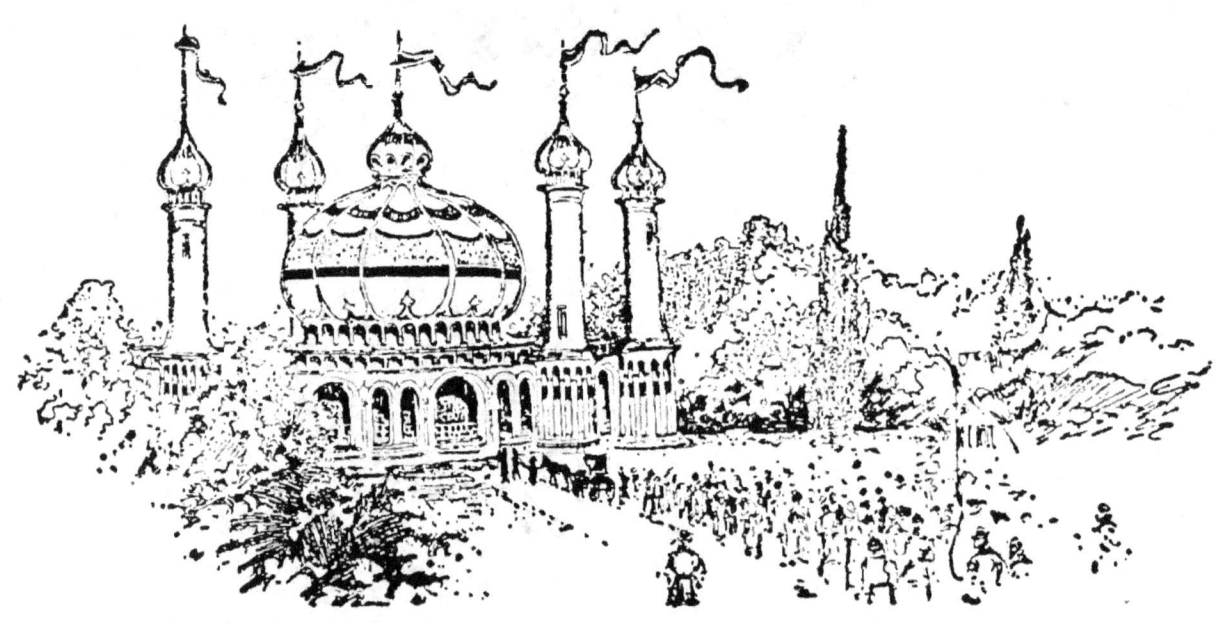

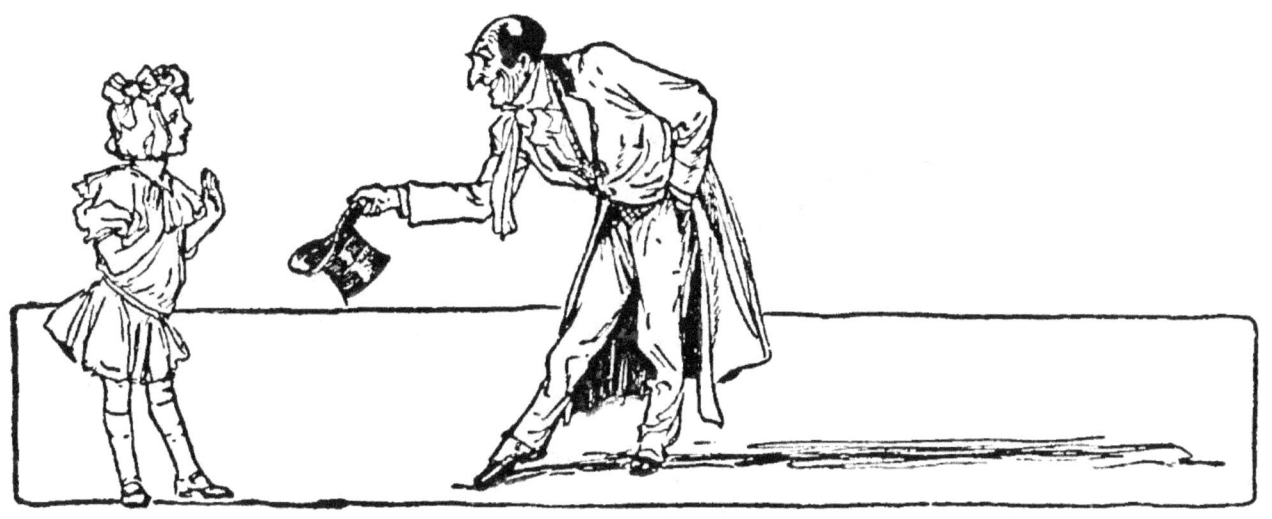

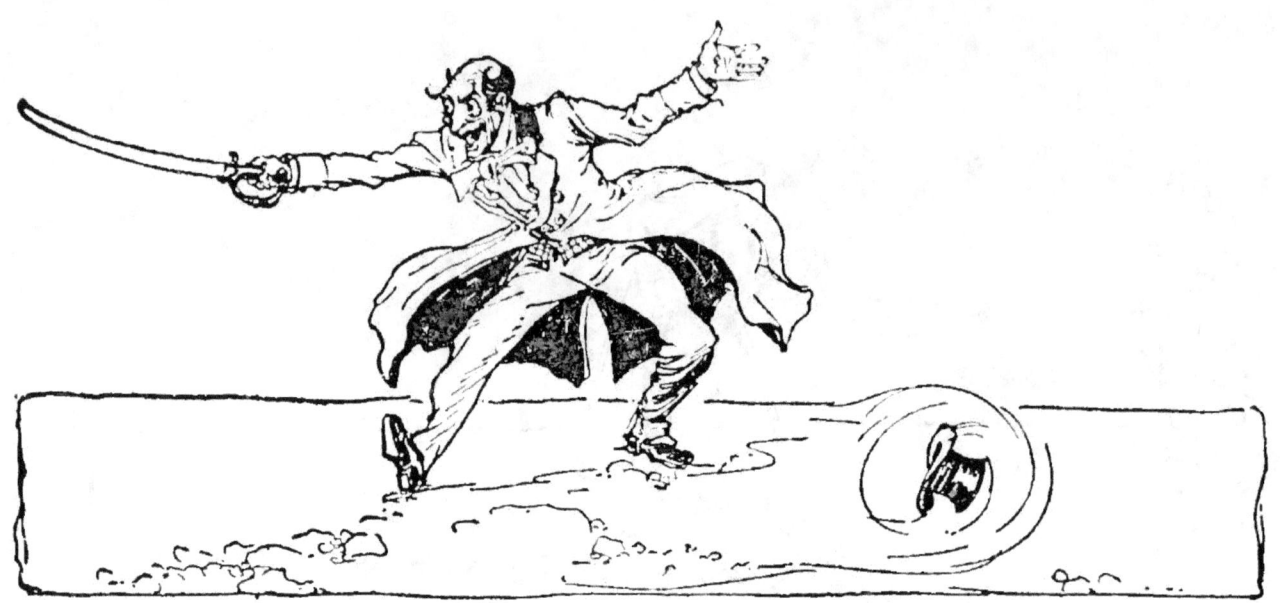

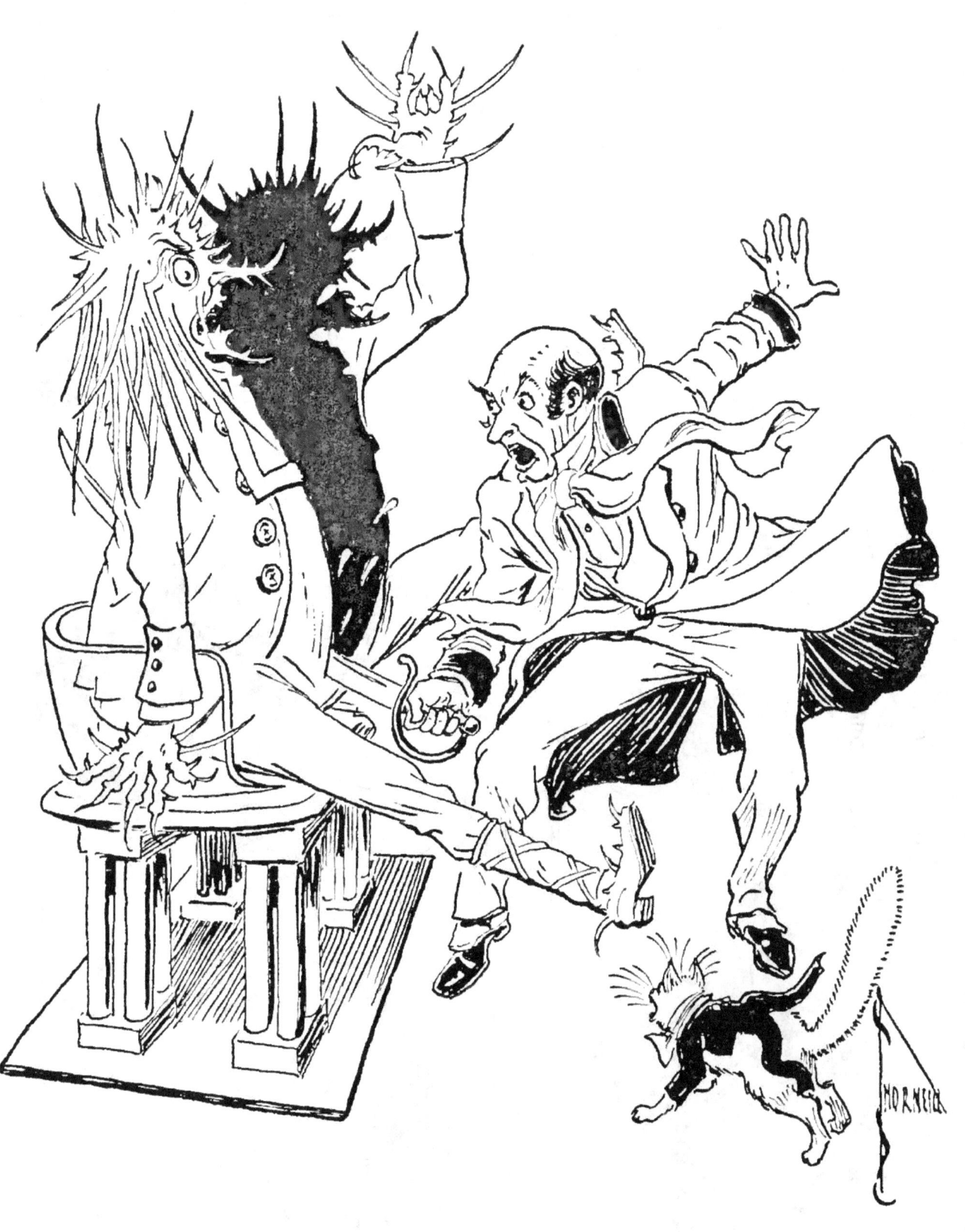

THE WIZARD CUT THE SORCERER EXACTLY IN TWO

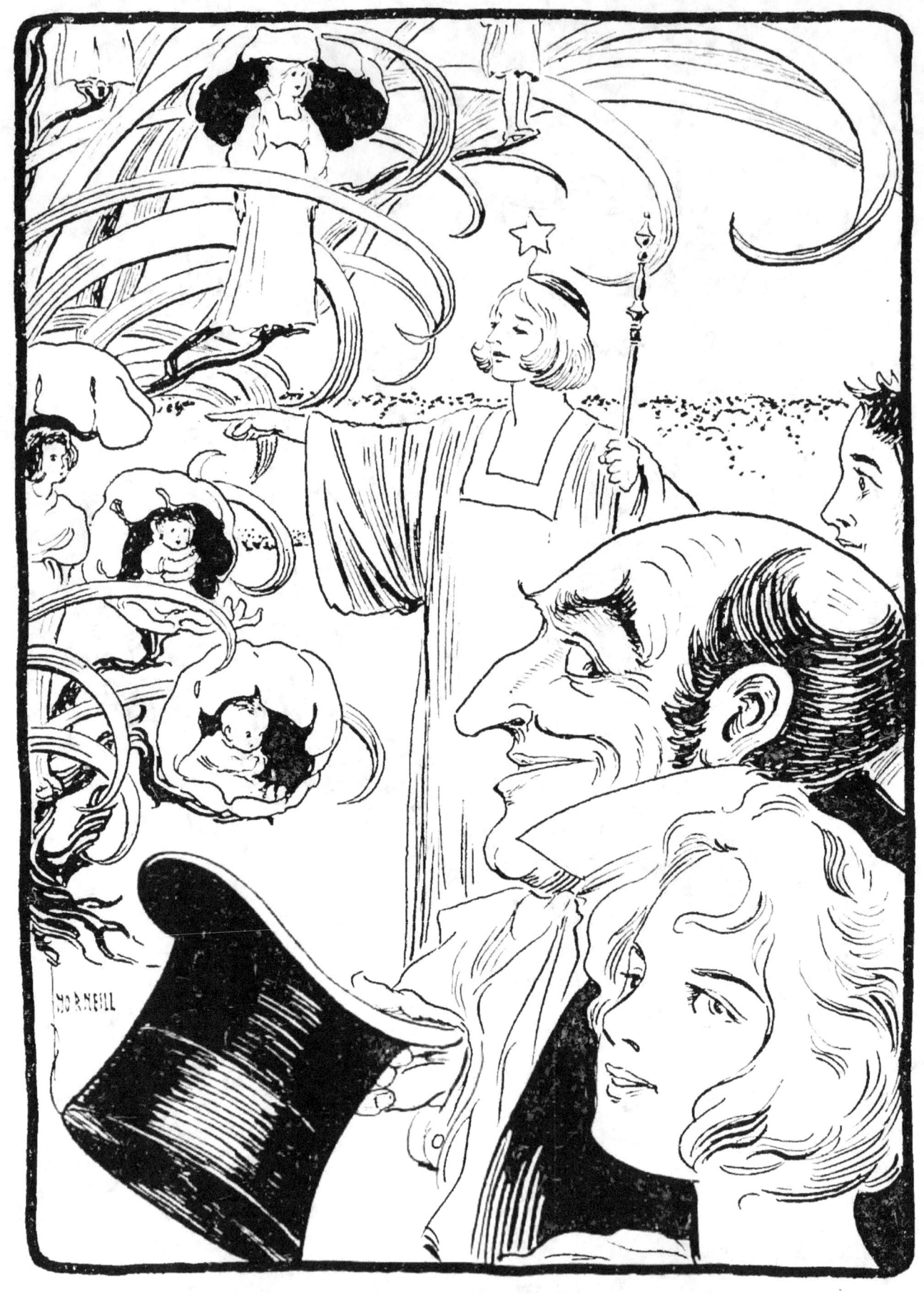

IN THE GARDEN OF THE MANGABOOS

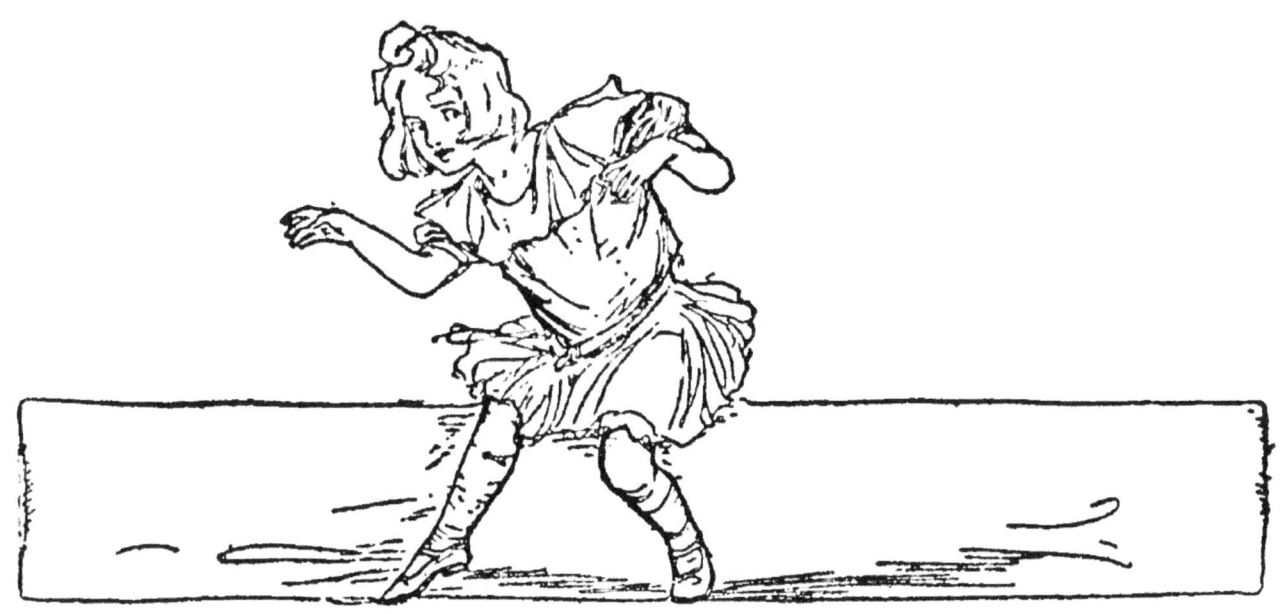

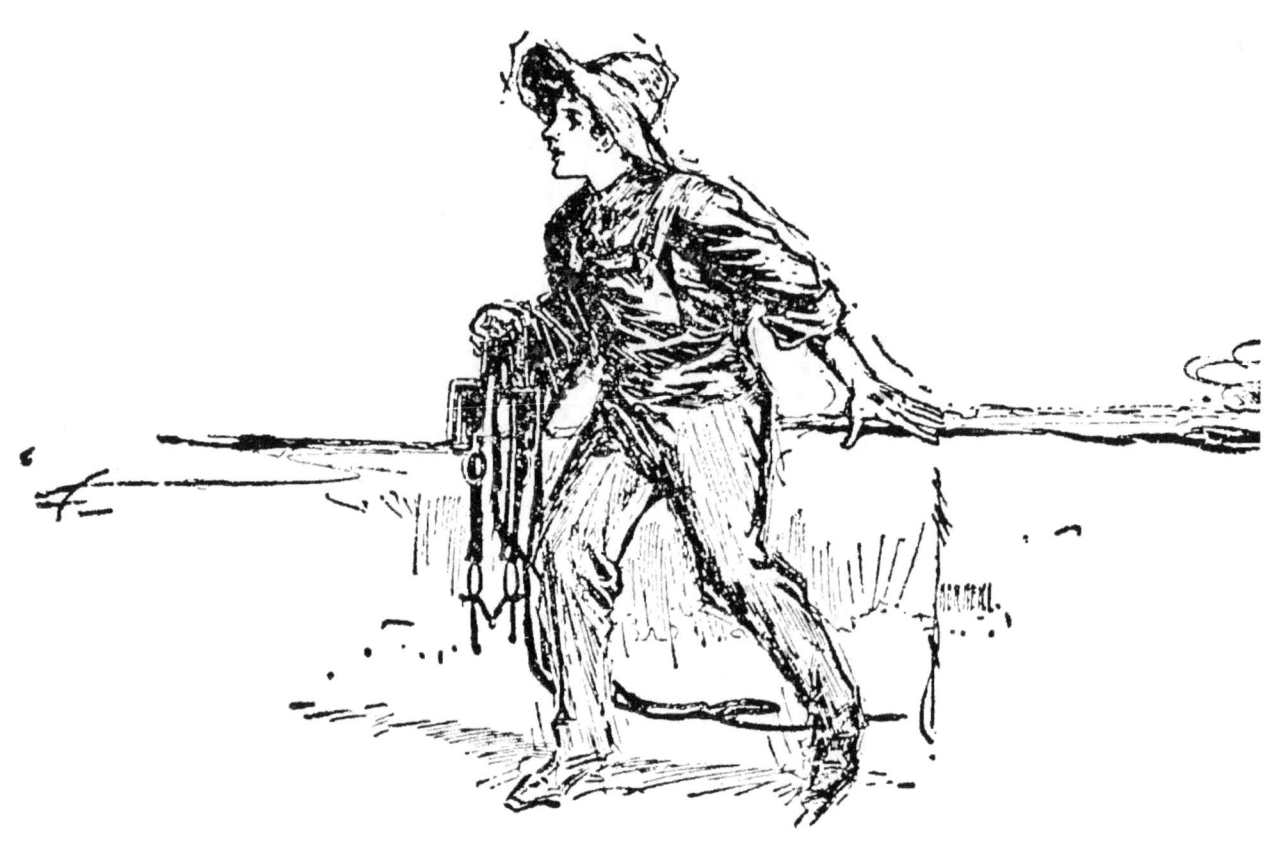

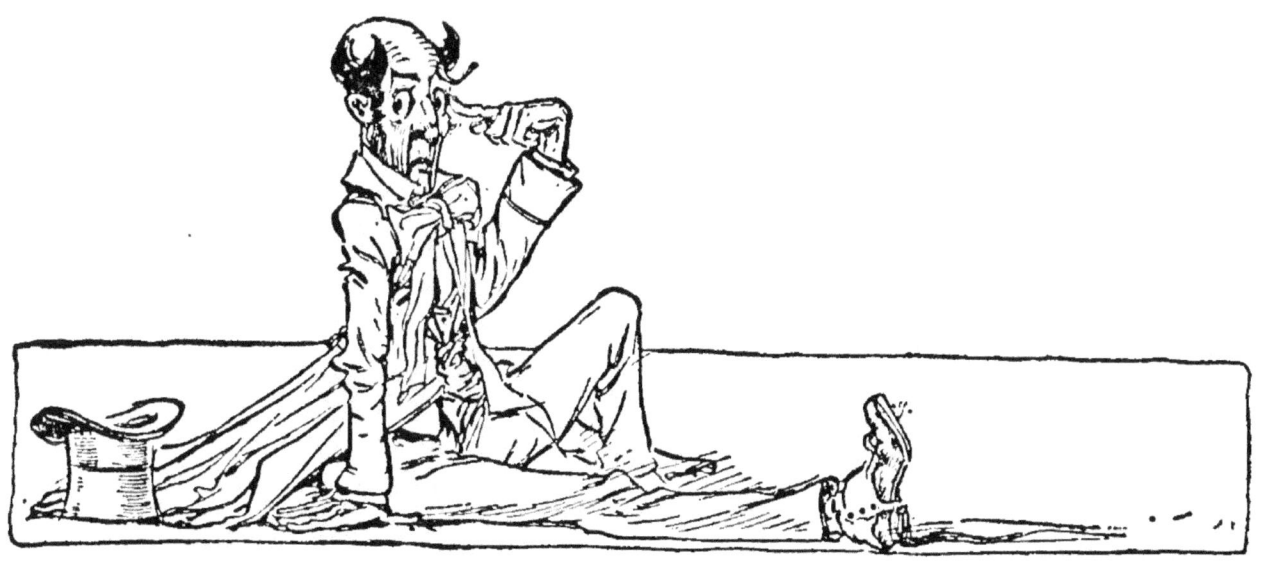

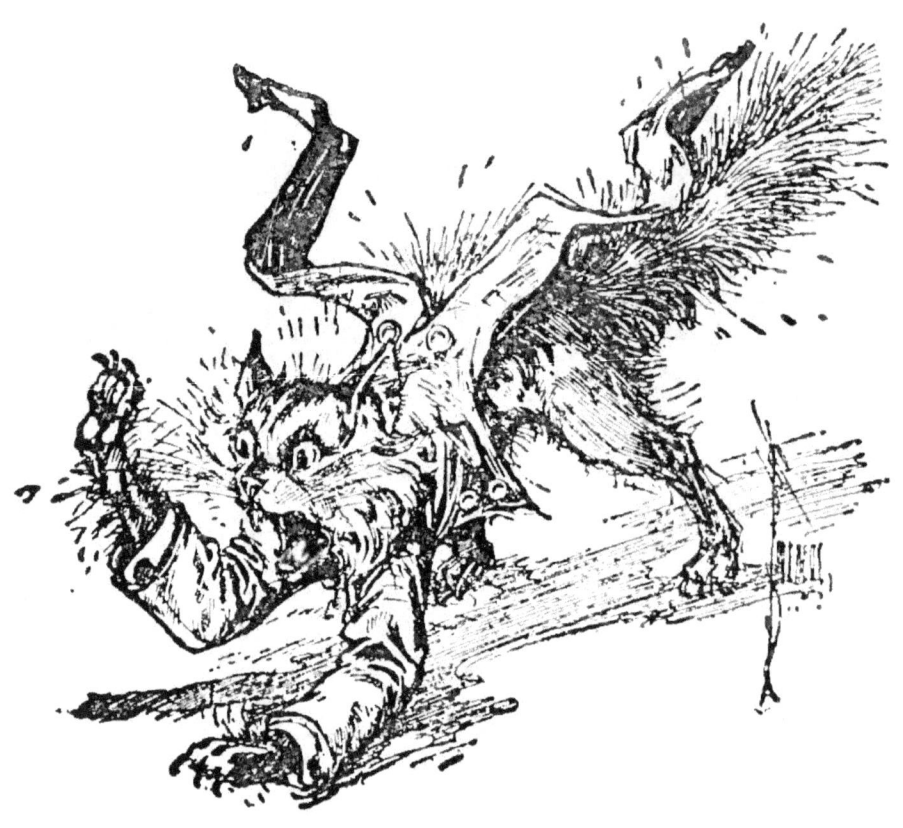

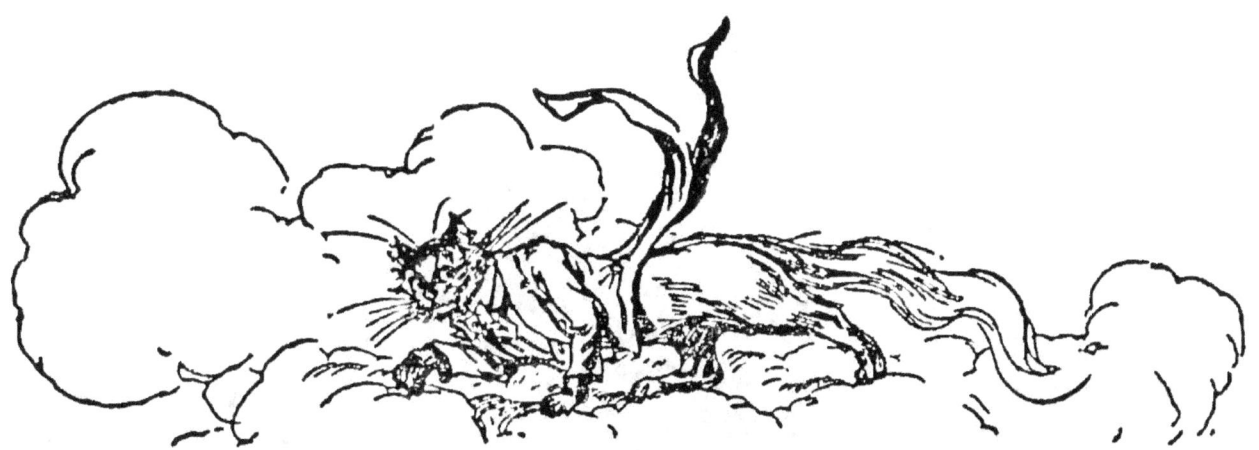

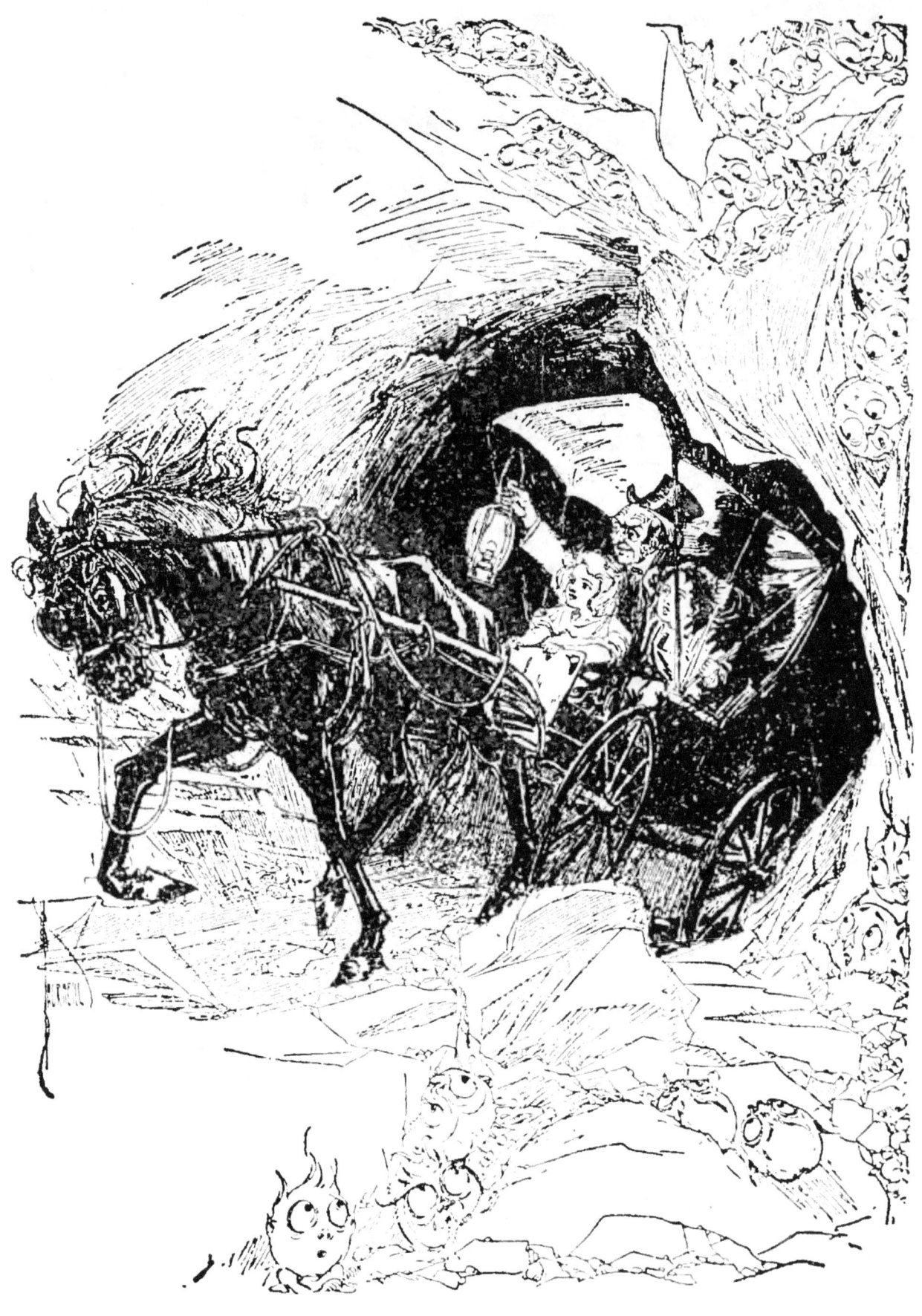

THROUGH THE BLACK PIT

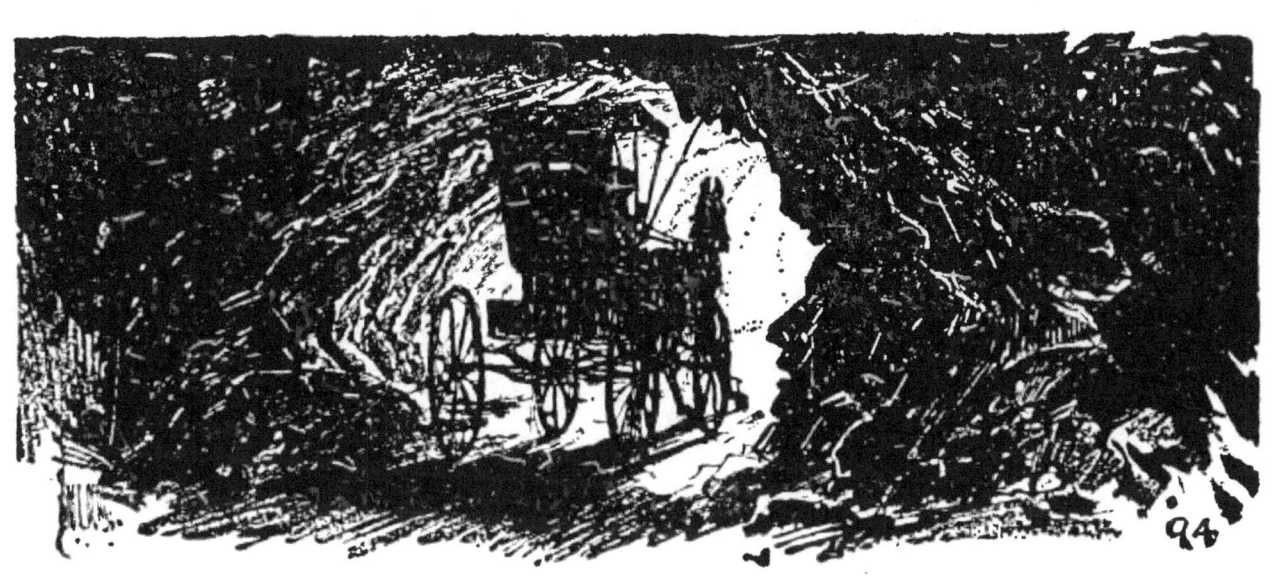

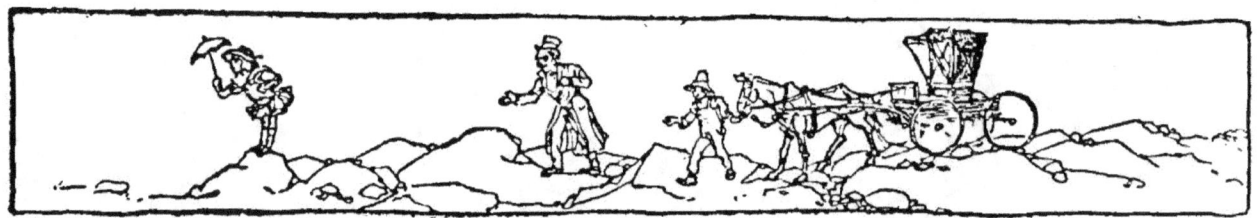

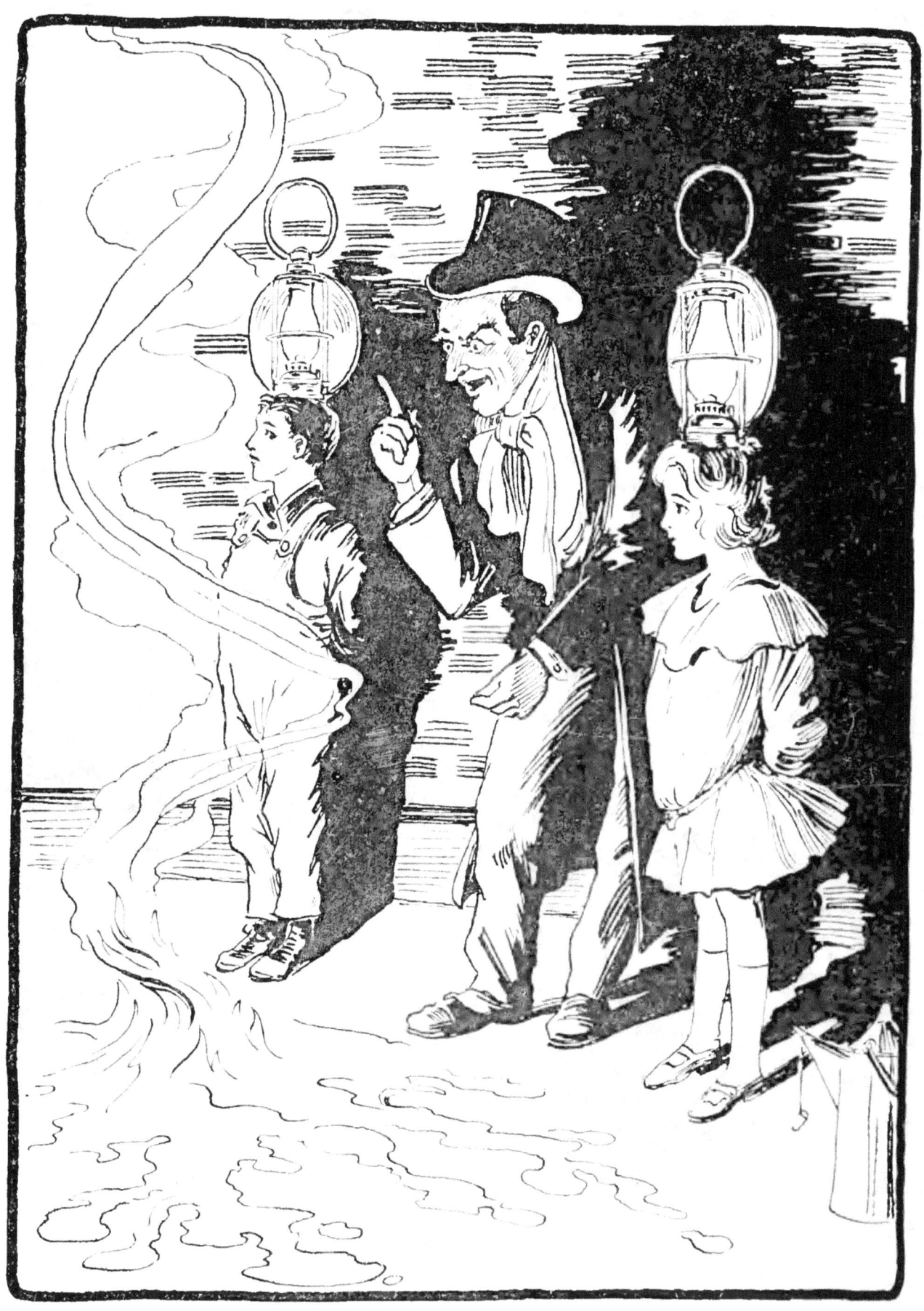

FOOLING THE MANGABOOS WITH FIRE

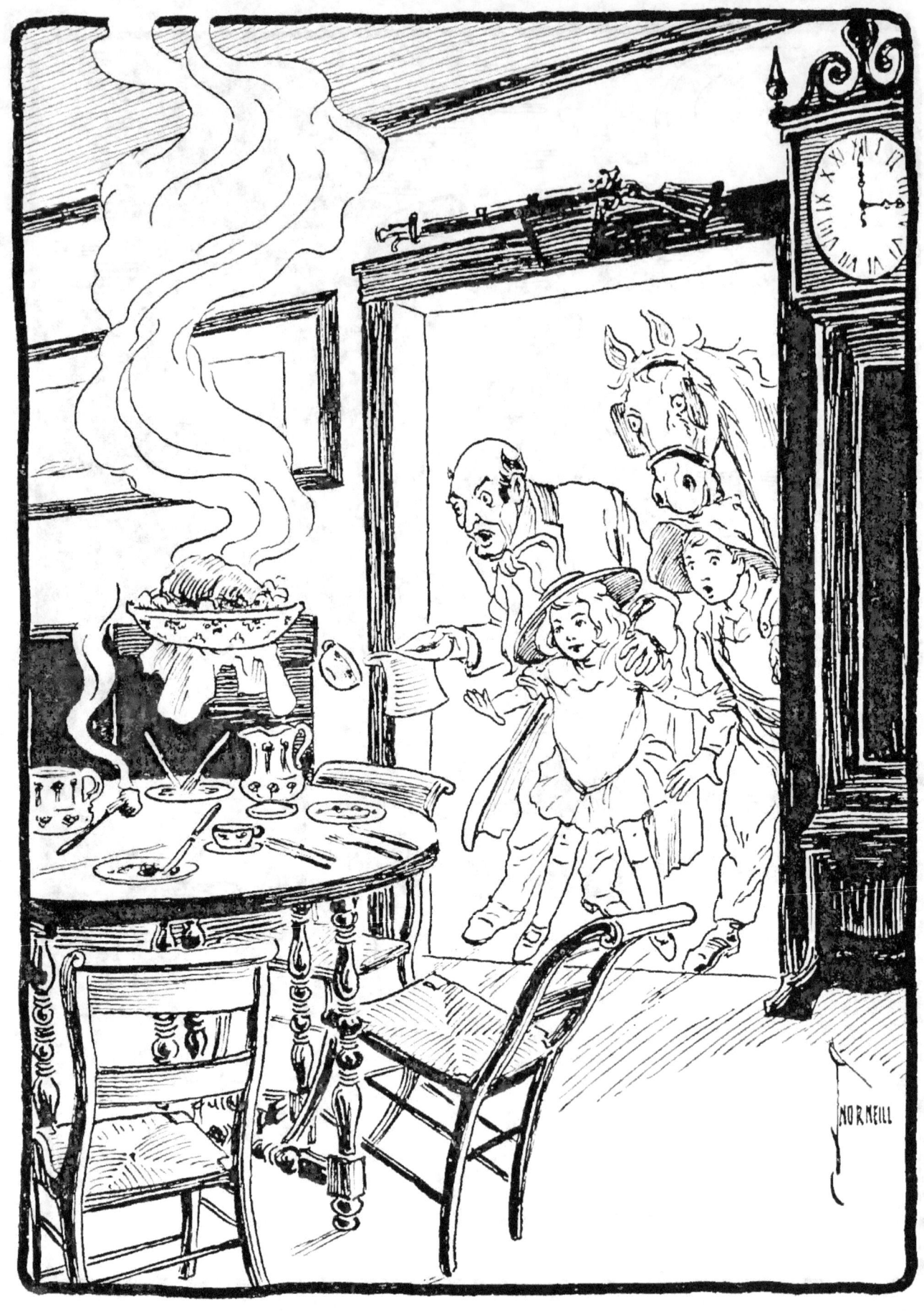

THE INVISIBLE PEOPLE OF VOE

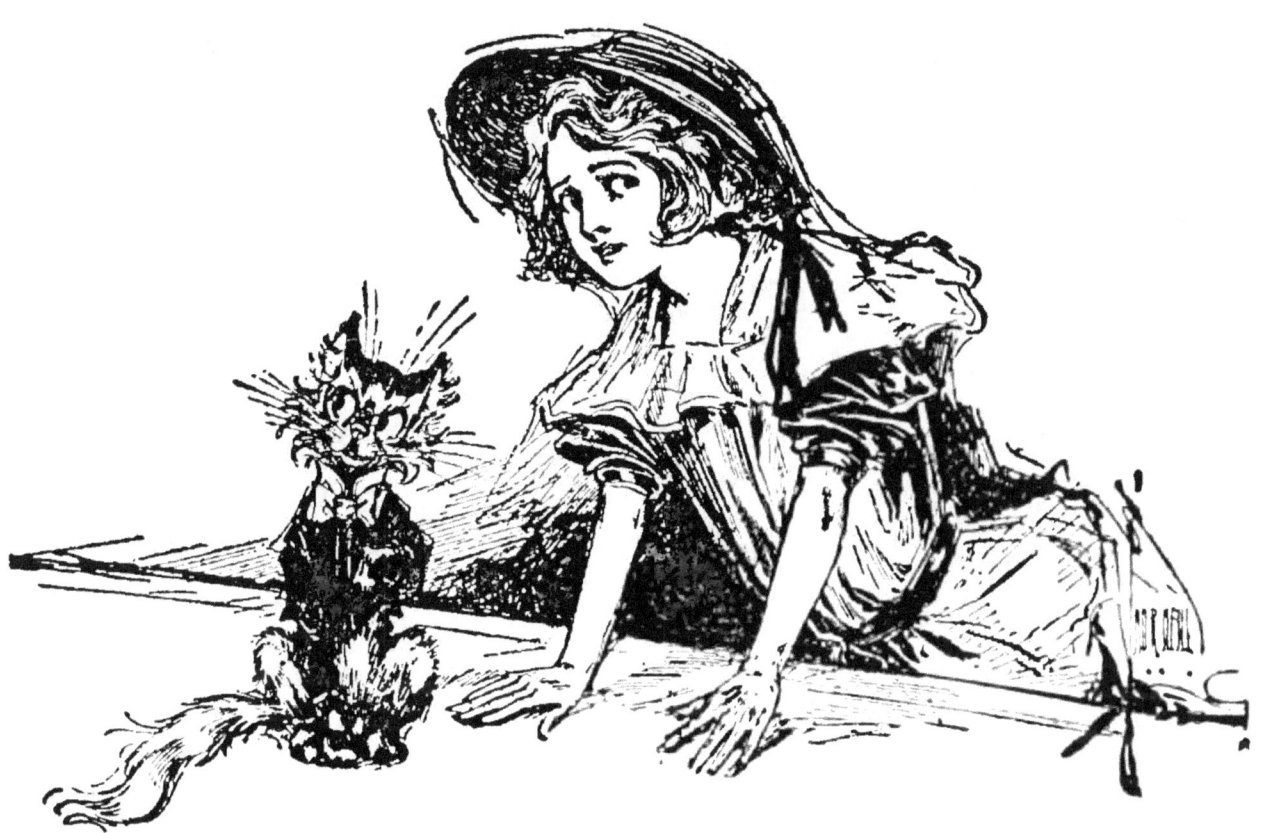

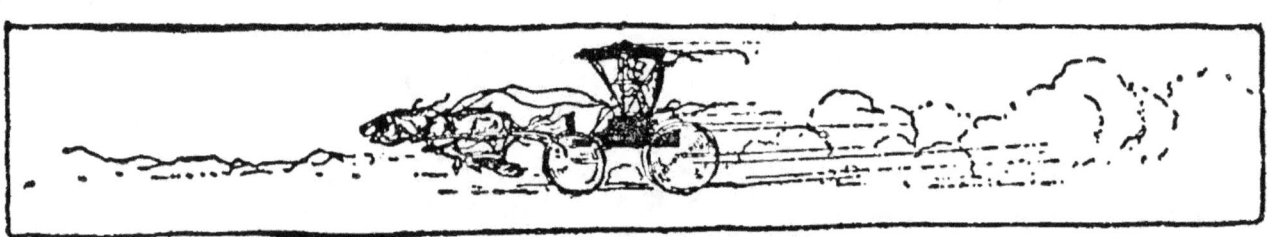

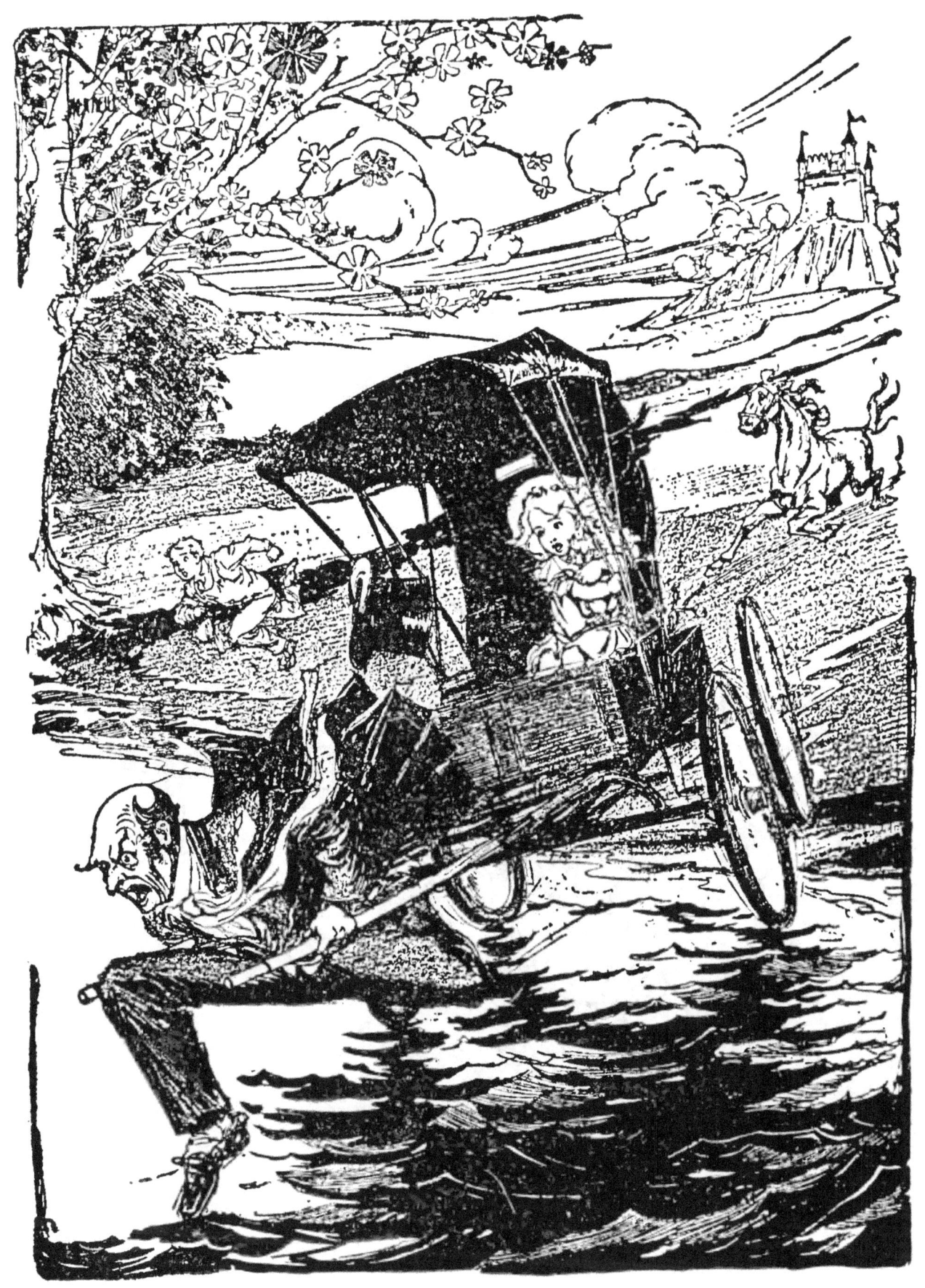

ESCAPING THE INVISIBLE BEARS

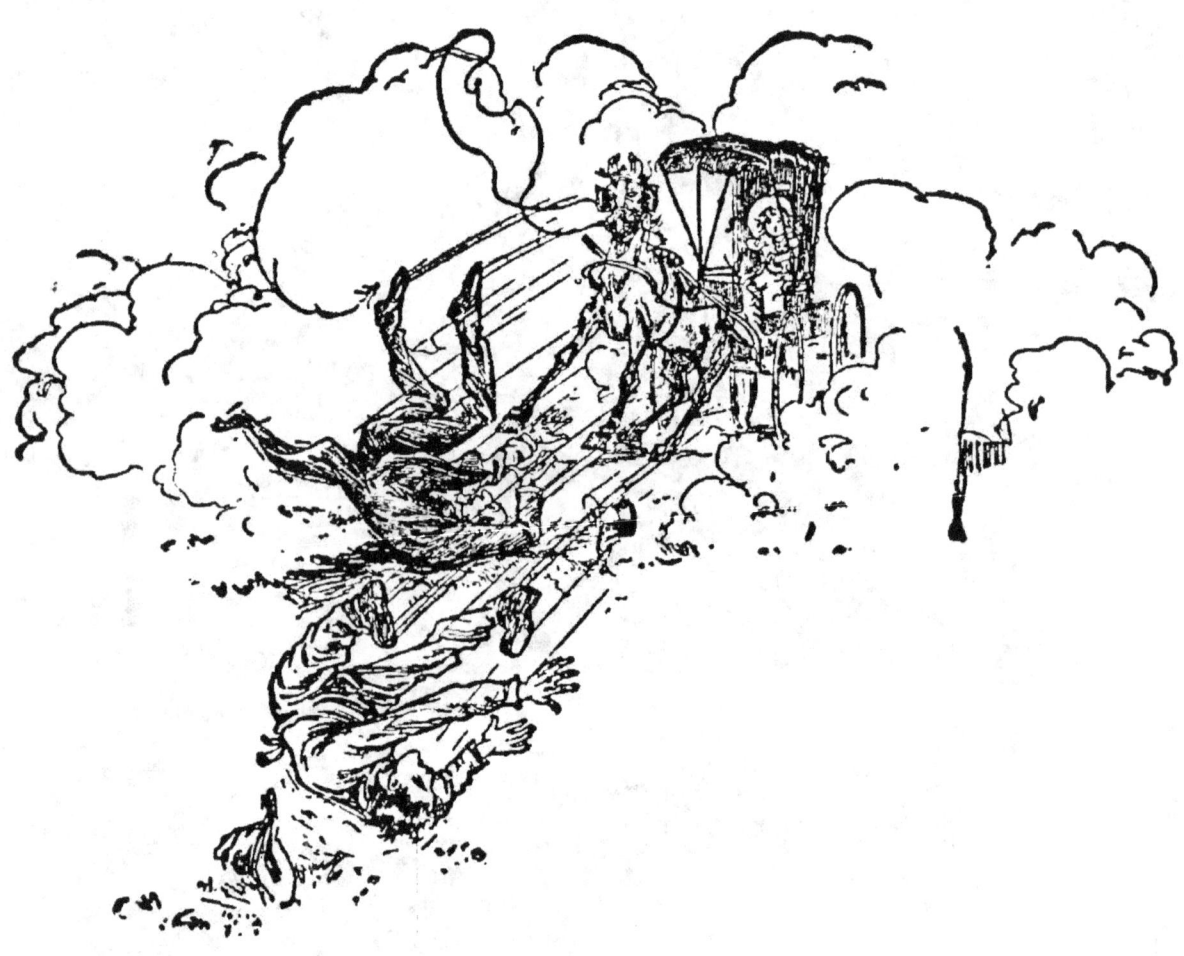

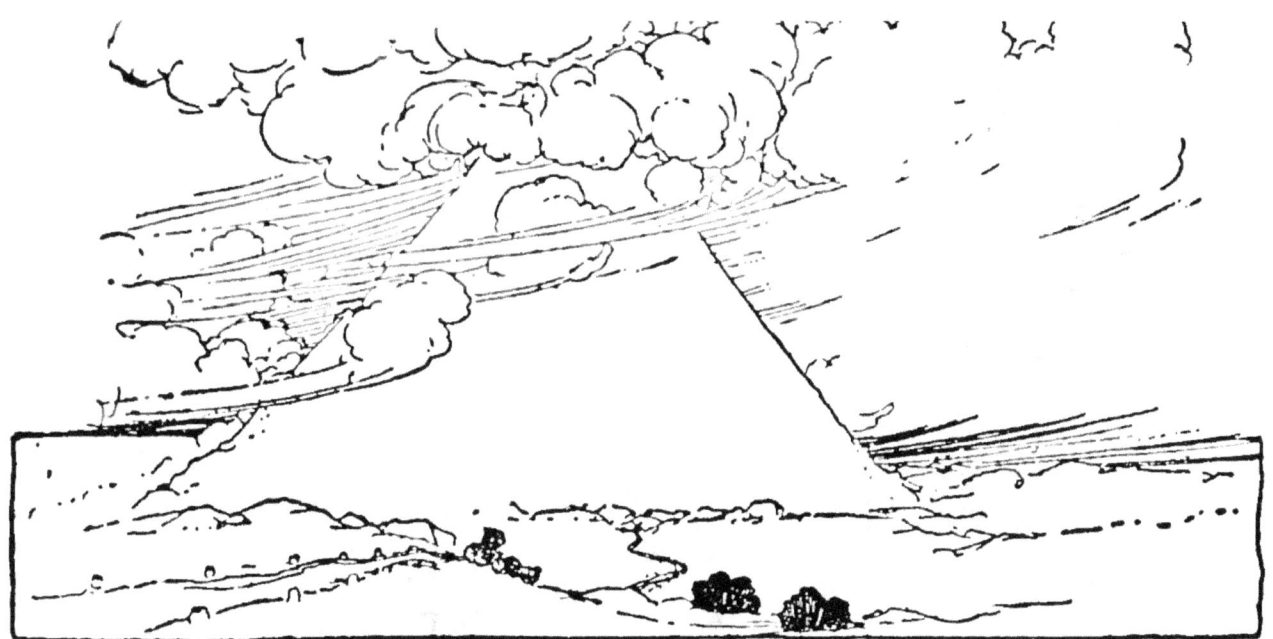

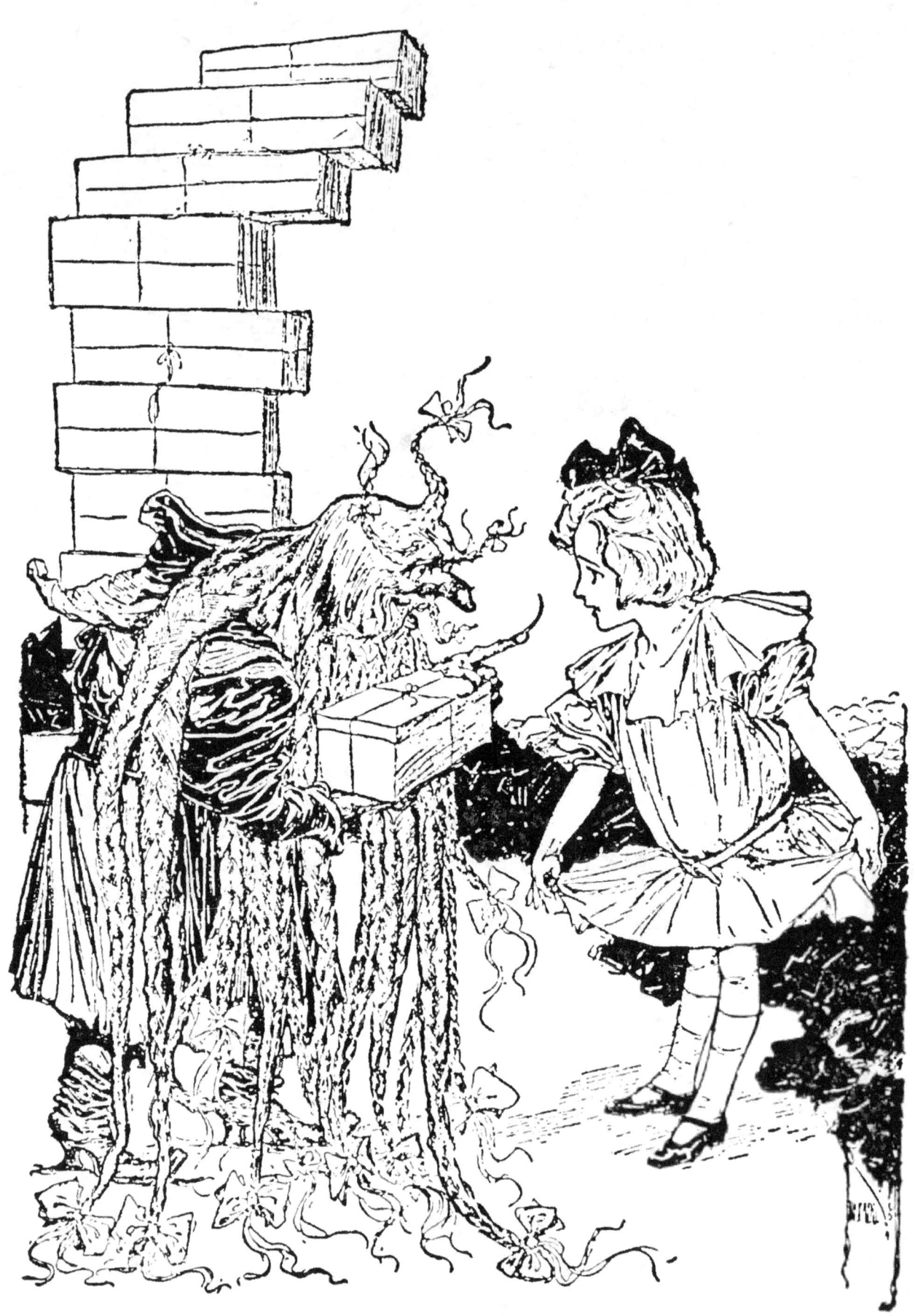

THE BRAIDED MAN

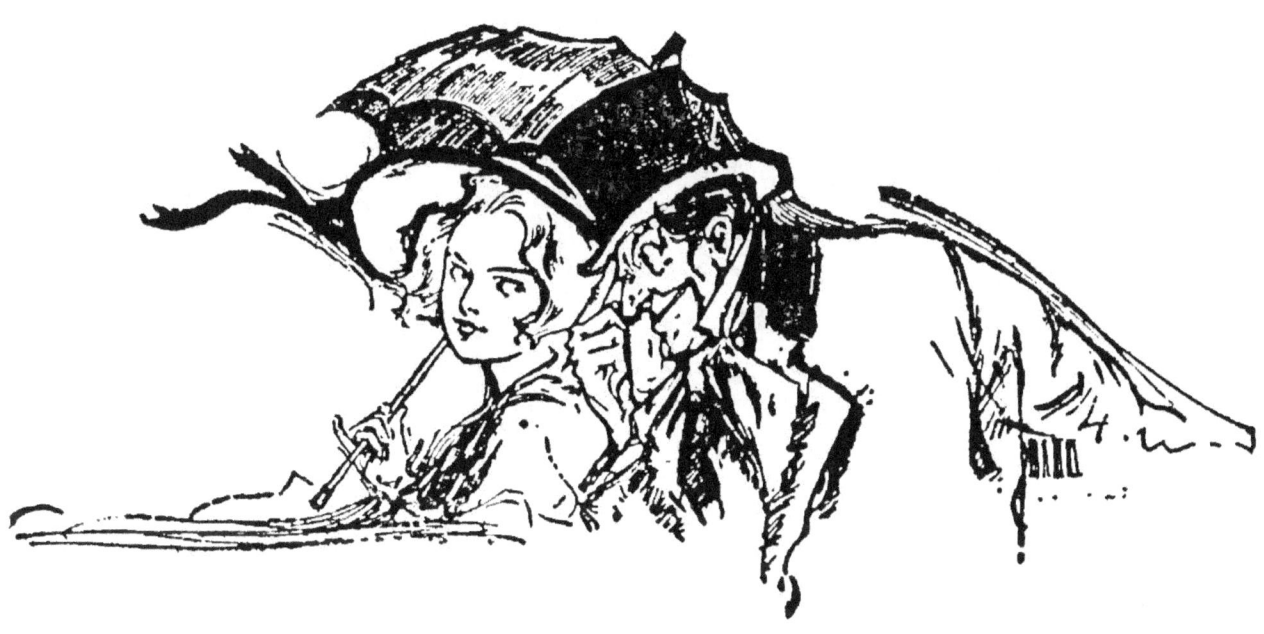

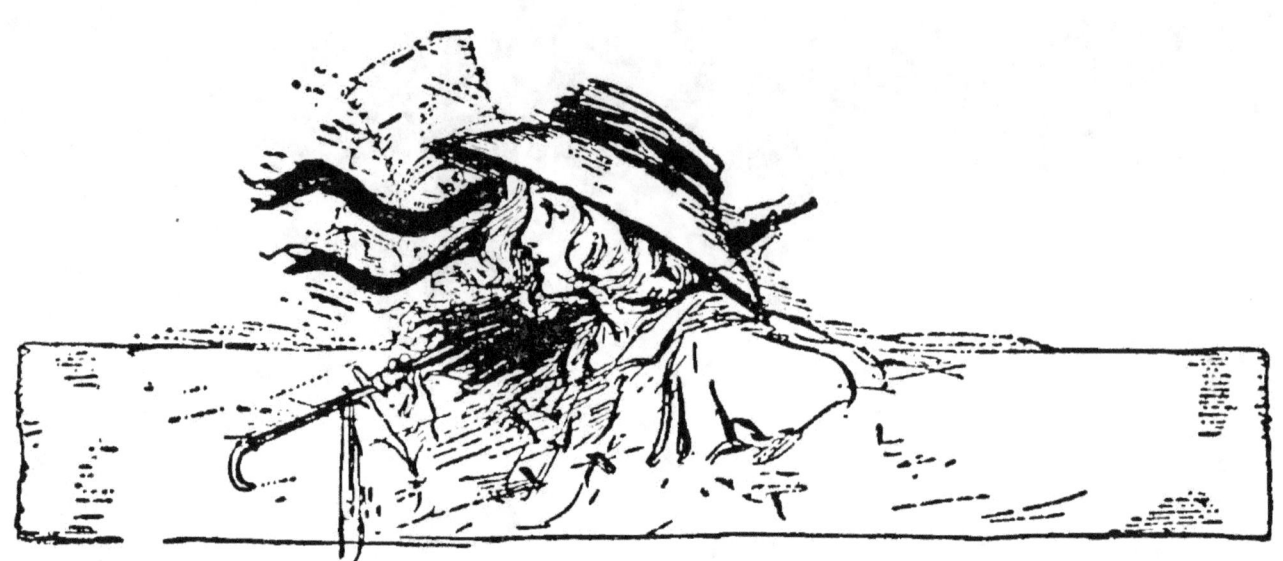

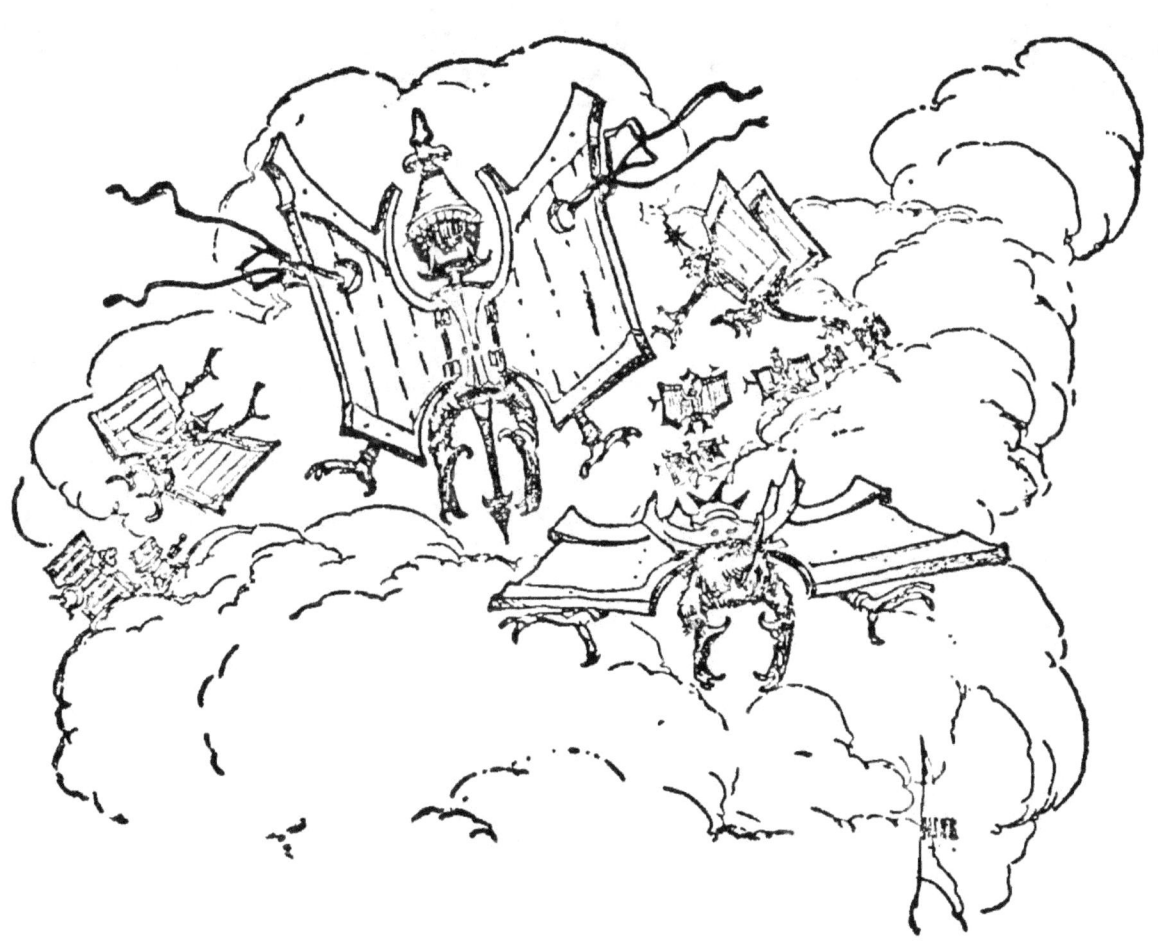

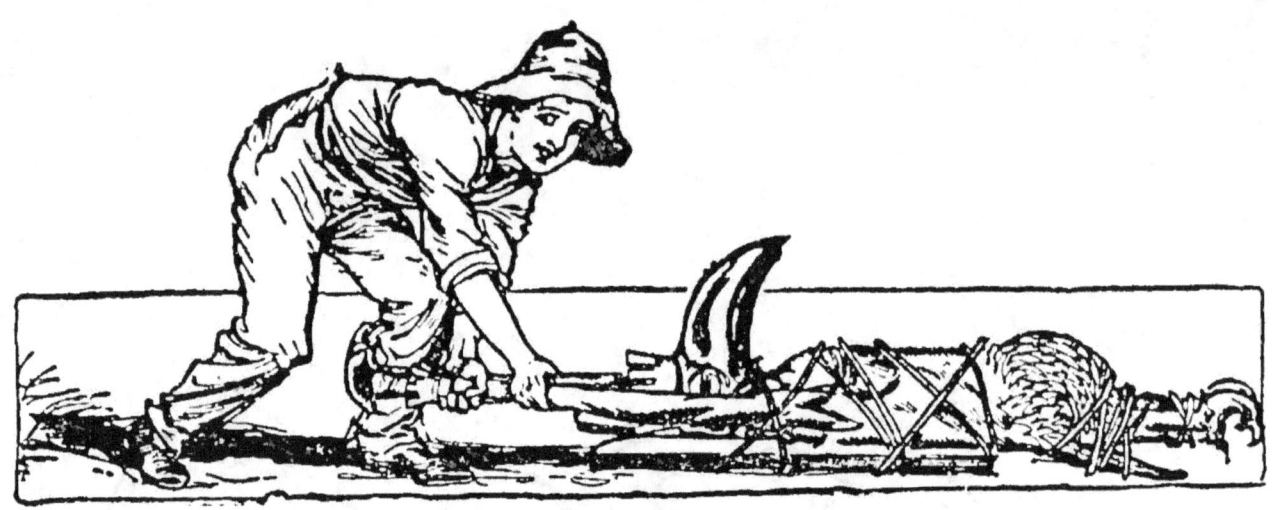

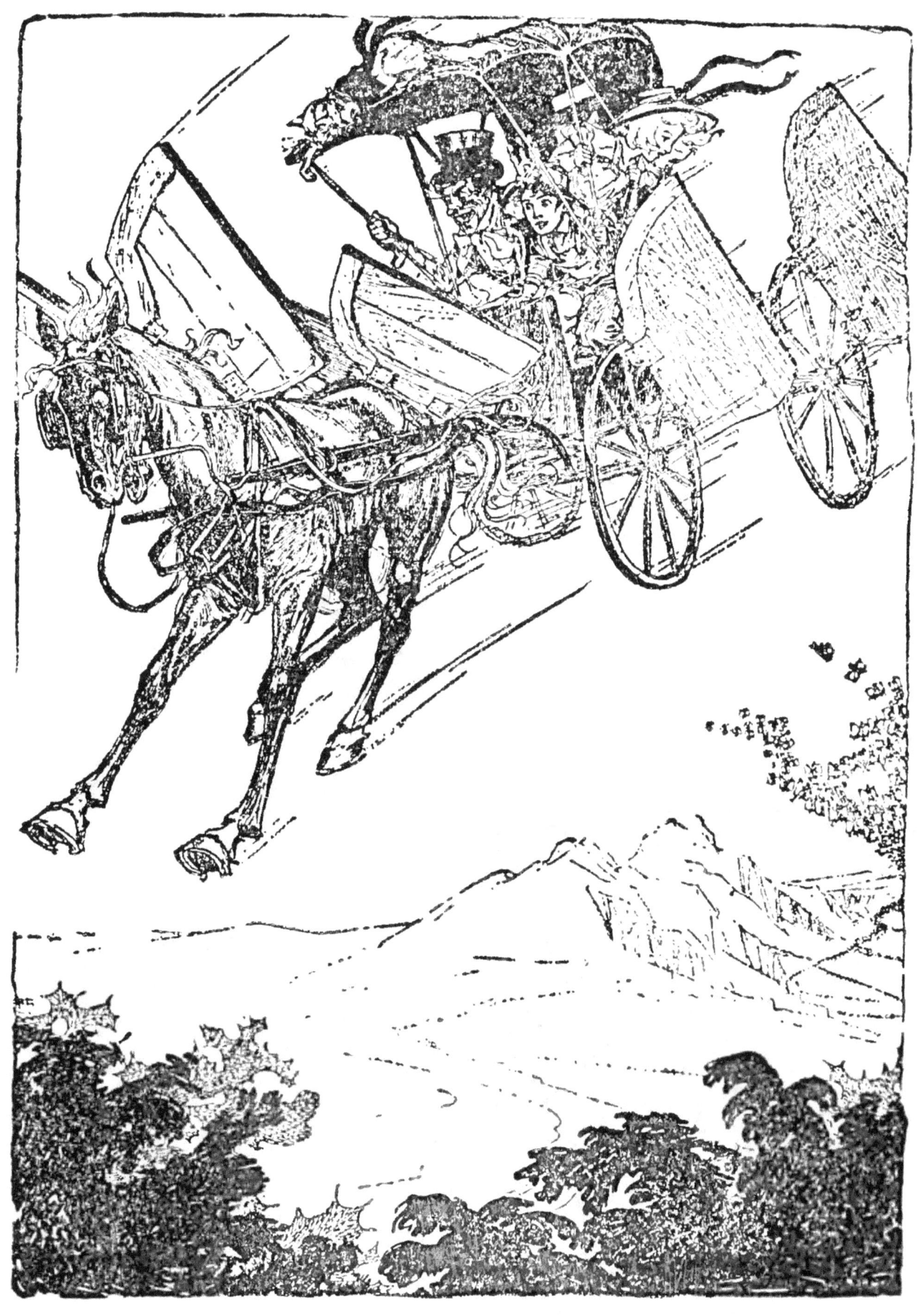

JIM FLOUNDERED THROUGH THE AIR

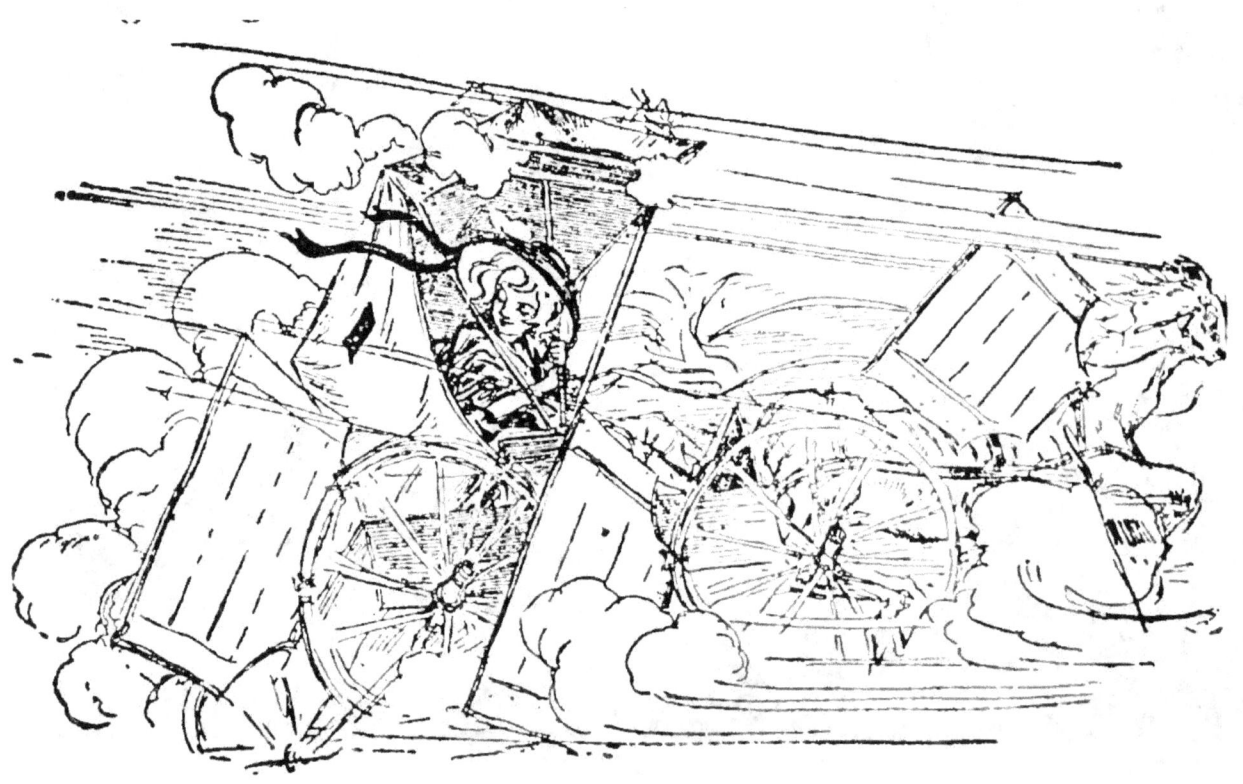

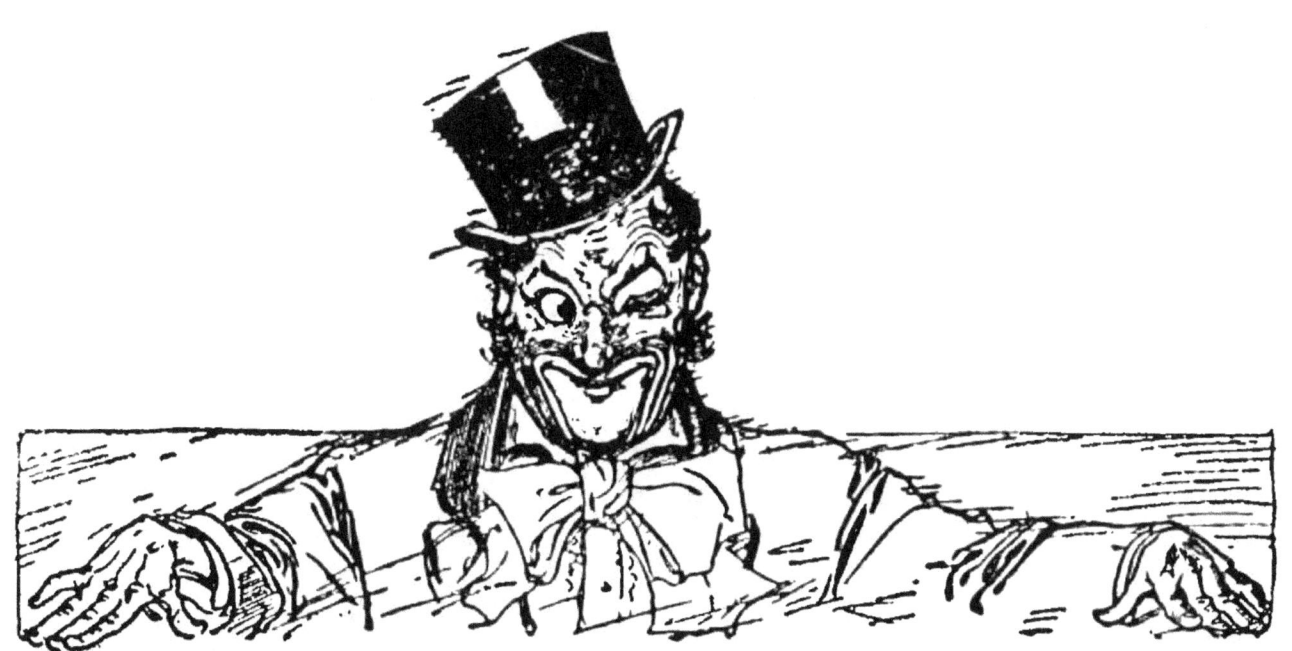

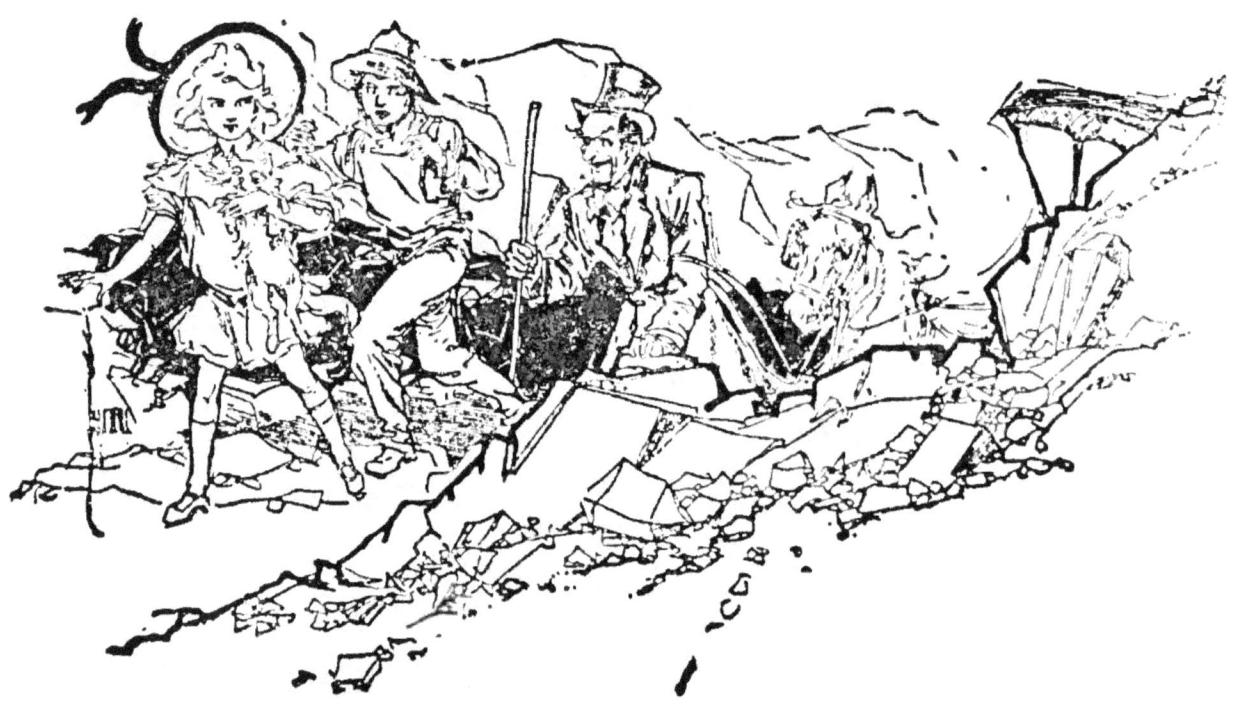

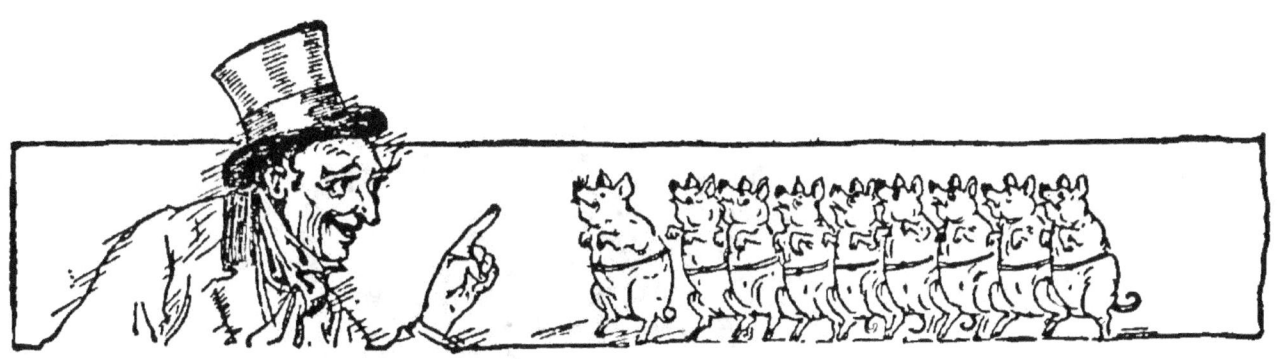

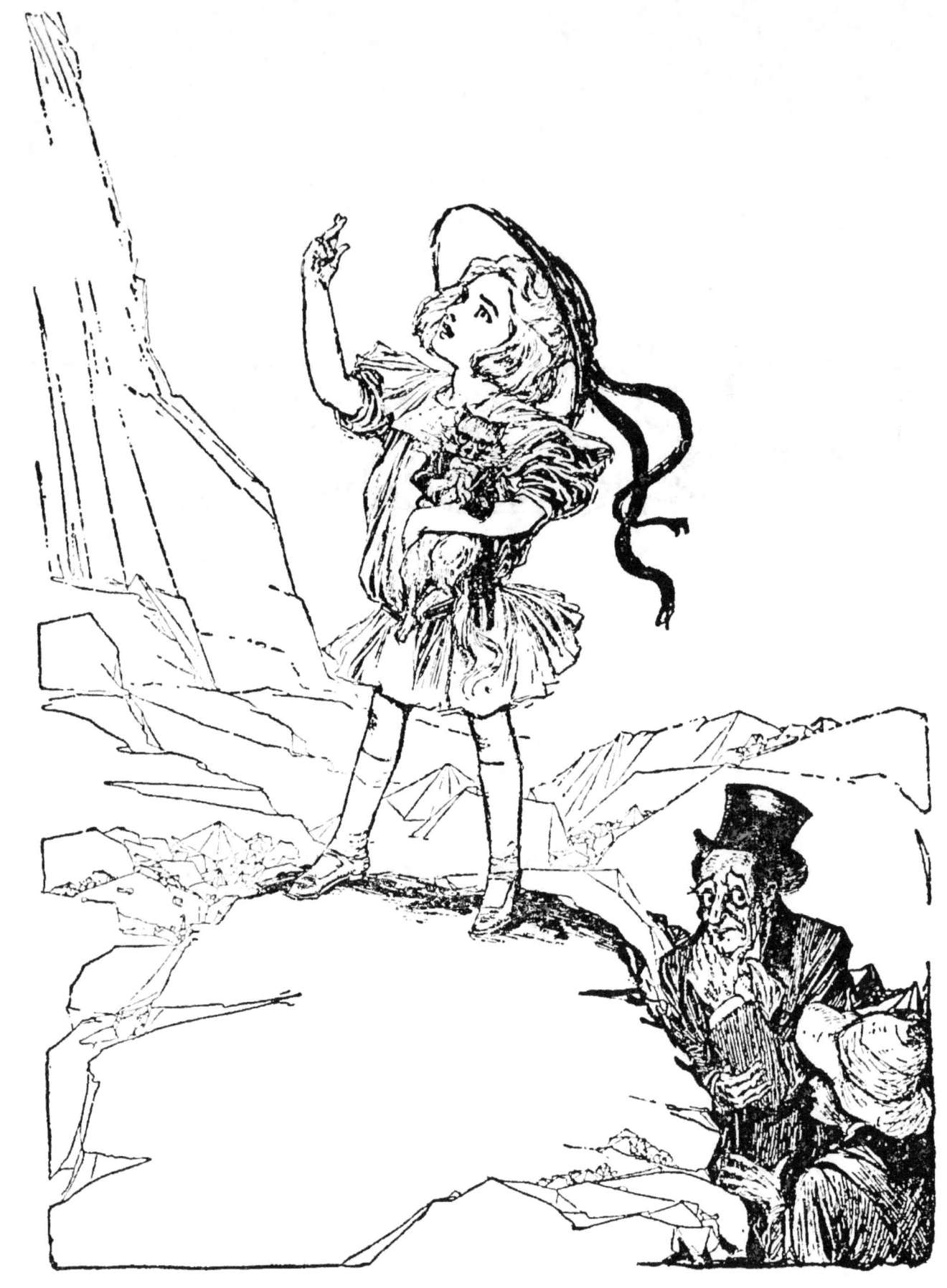

DOROTHY MADE THE SIGNAL

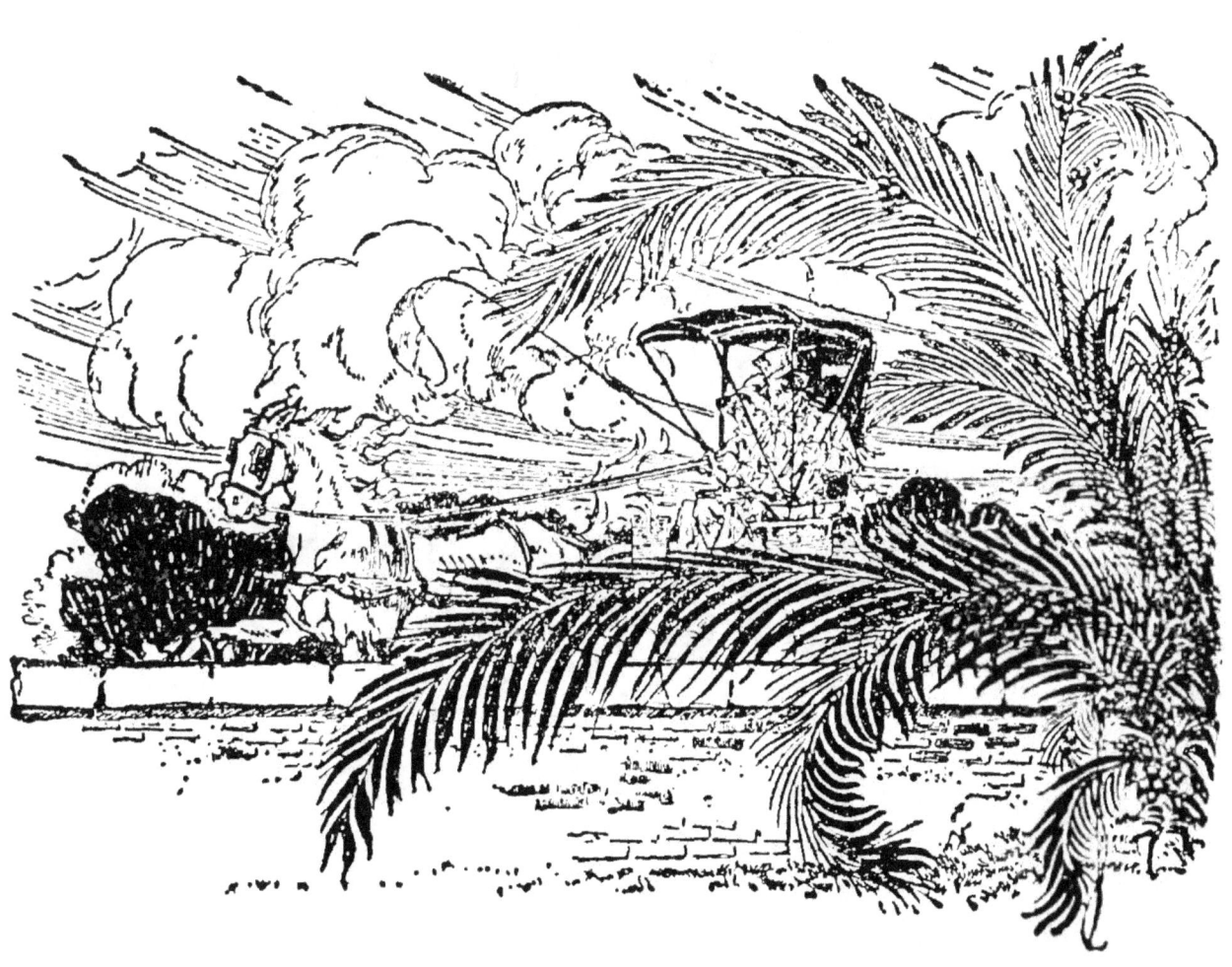

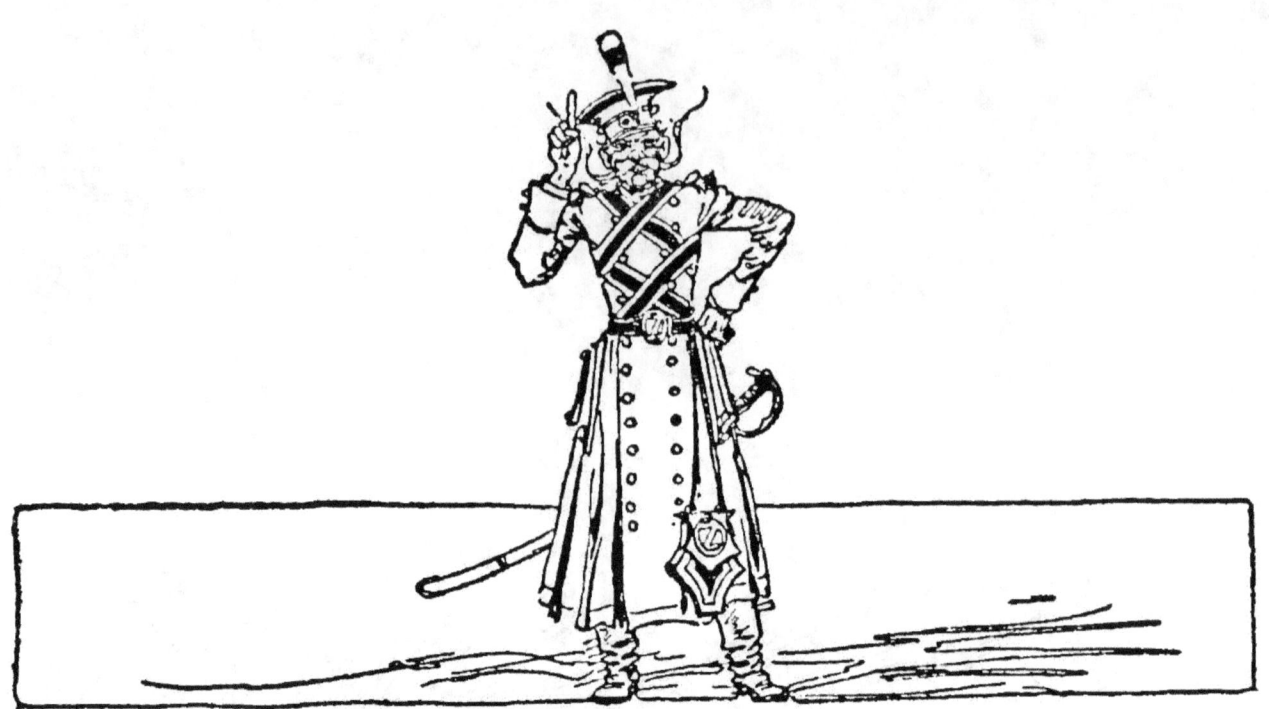

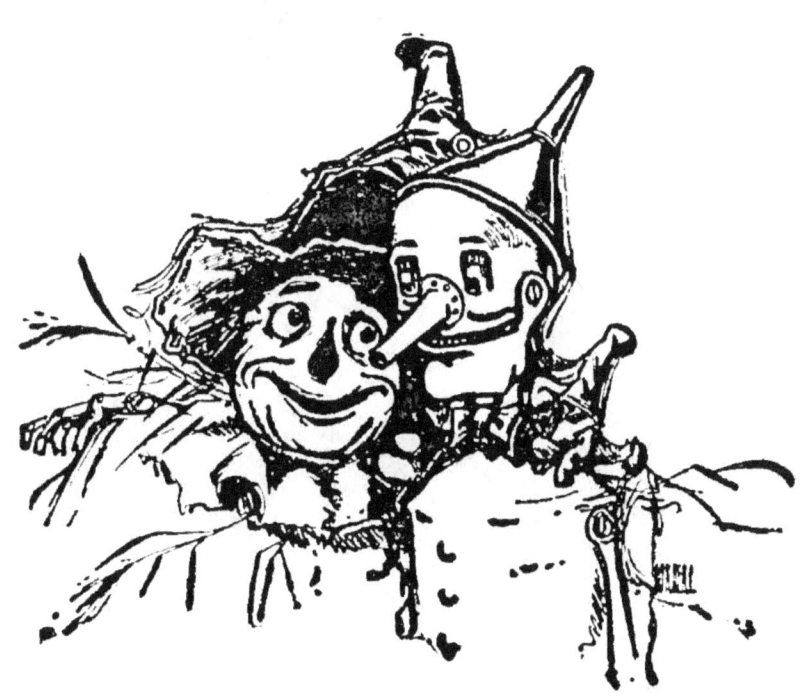

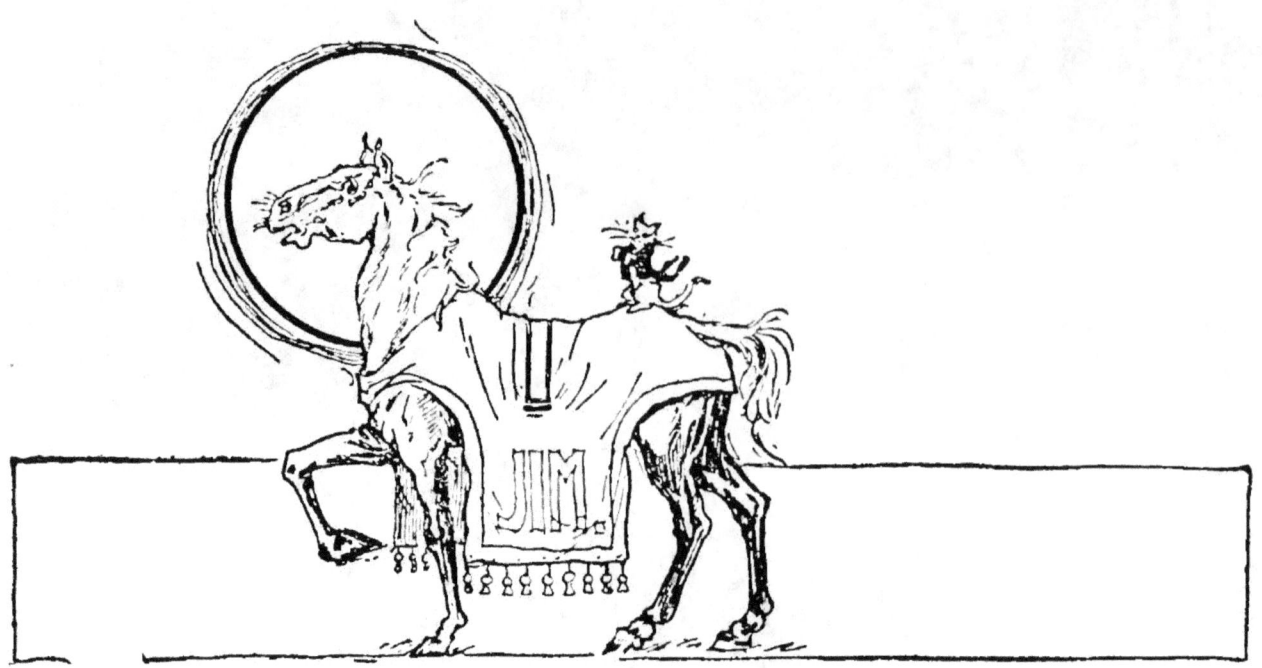

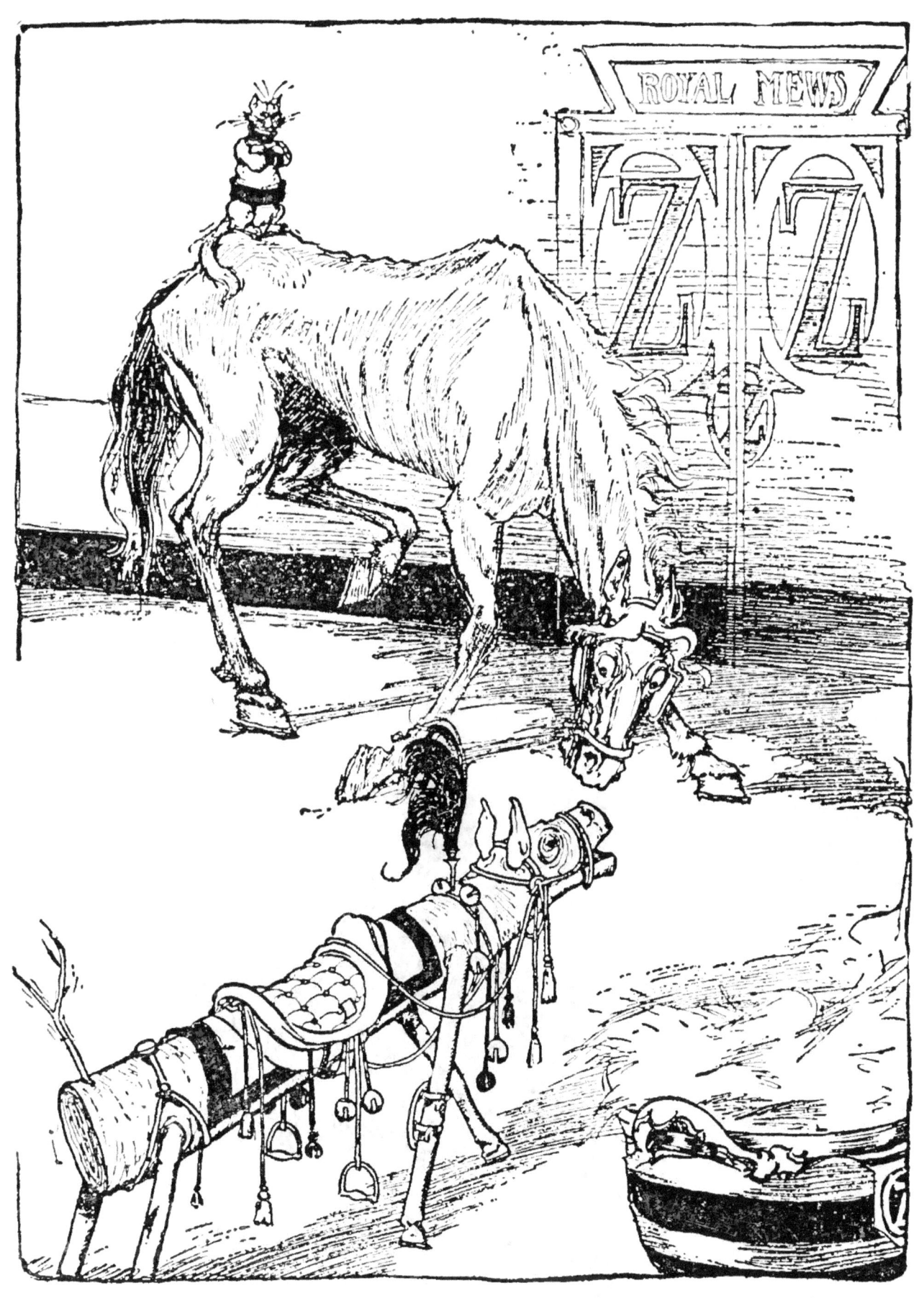

JIM STARED AT THE SAWHORSE

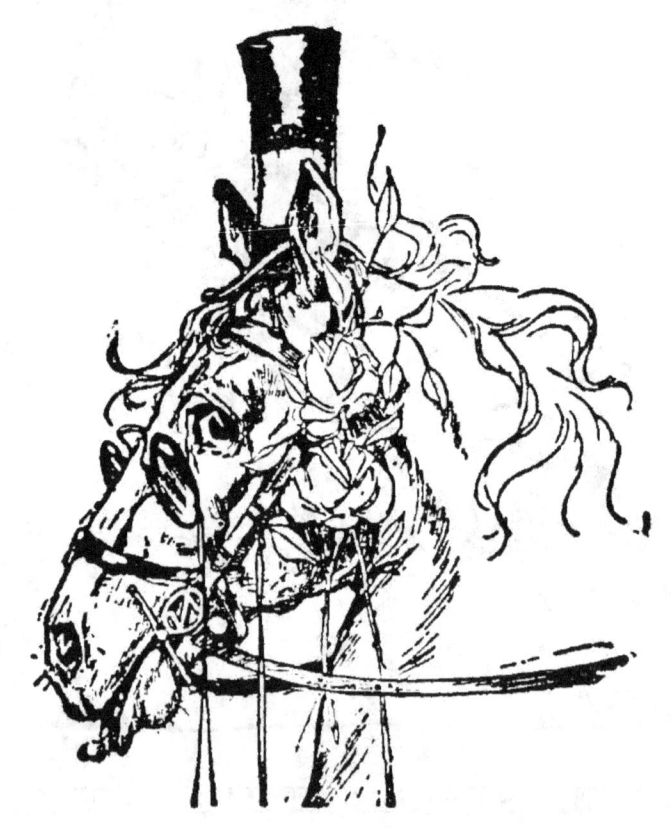

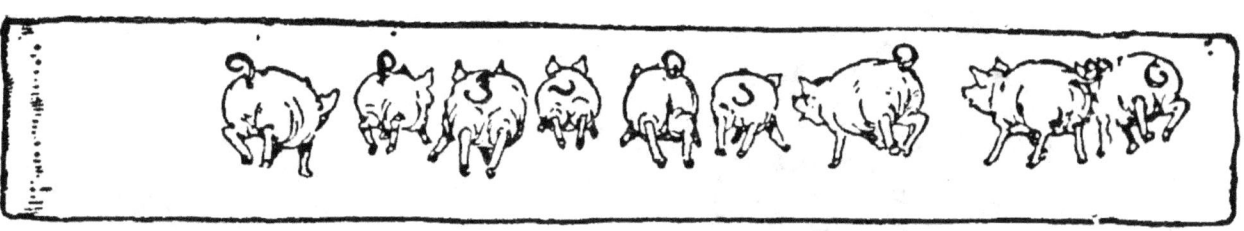

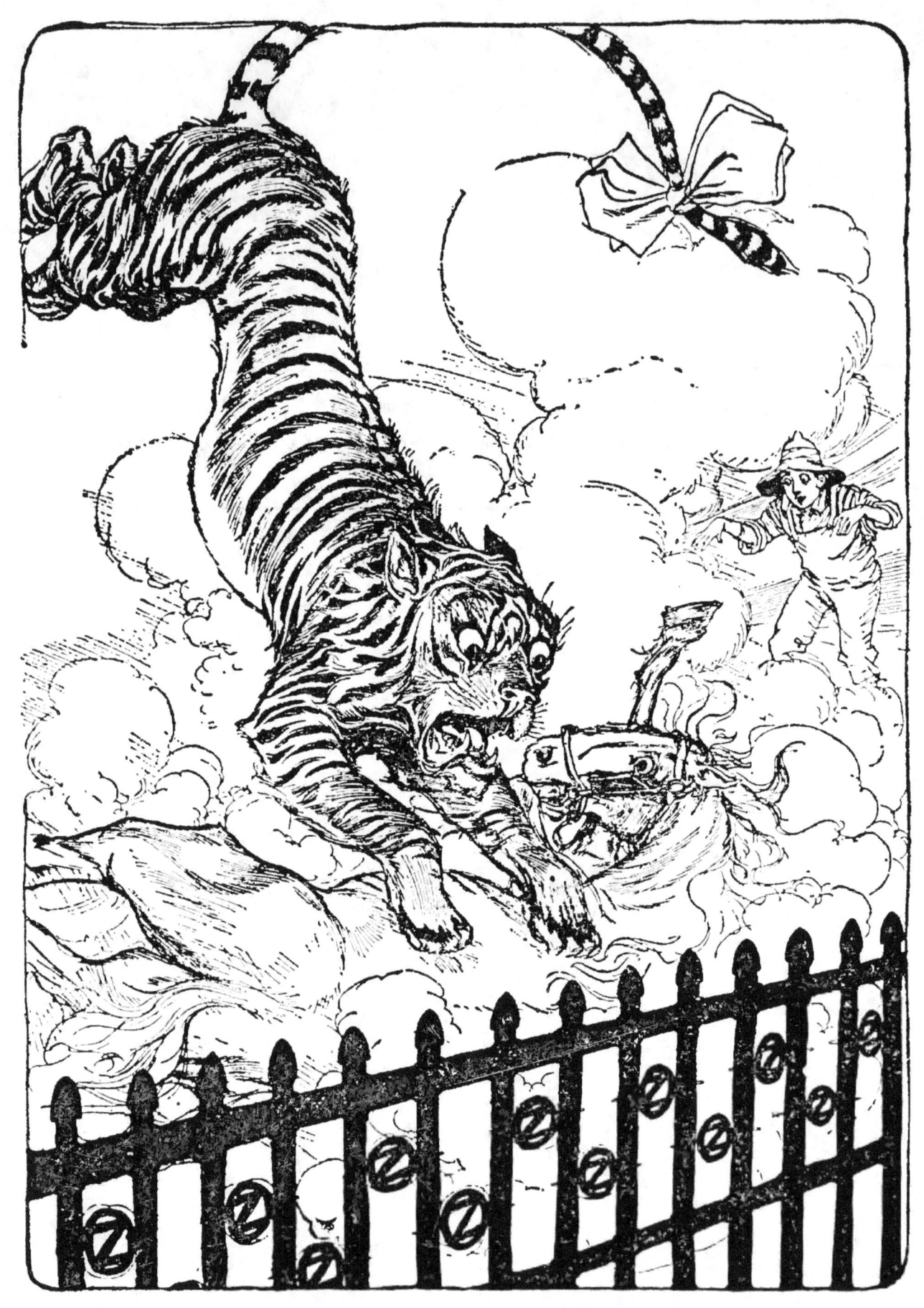

THE HUNGRY TIGER TEACHES JIM A LESSON

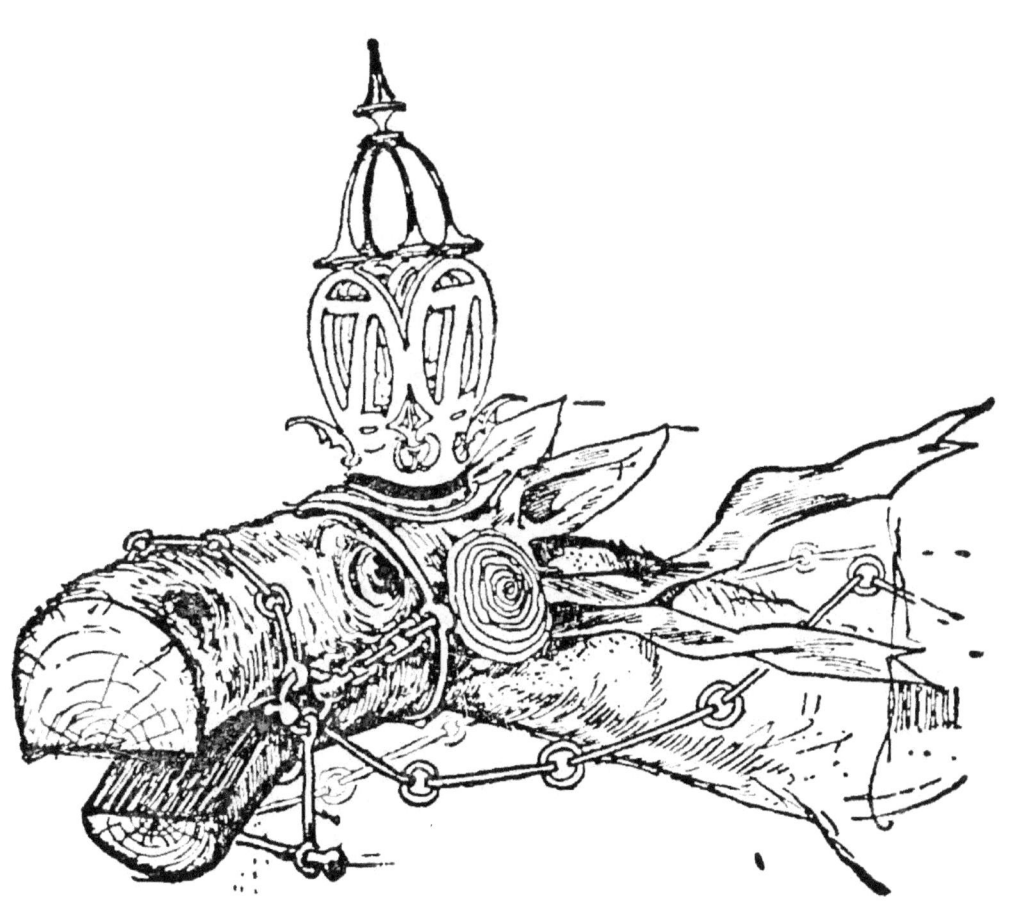

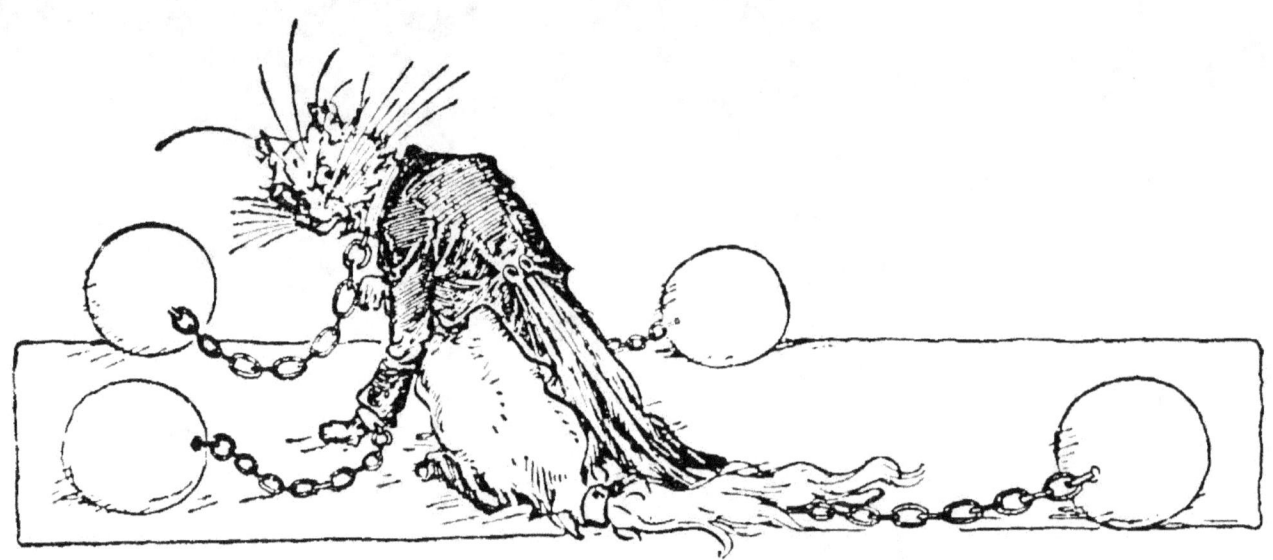

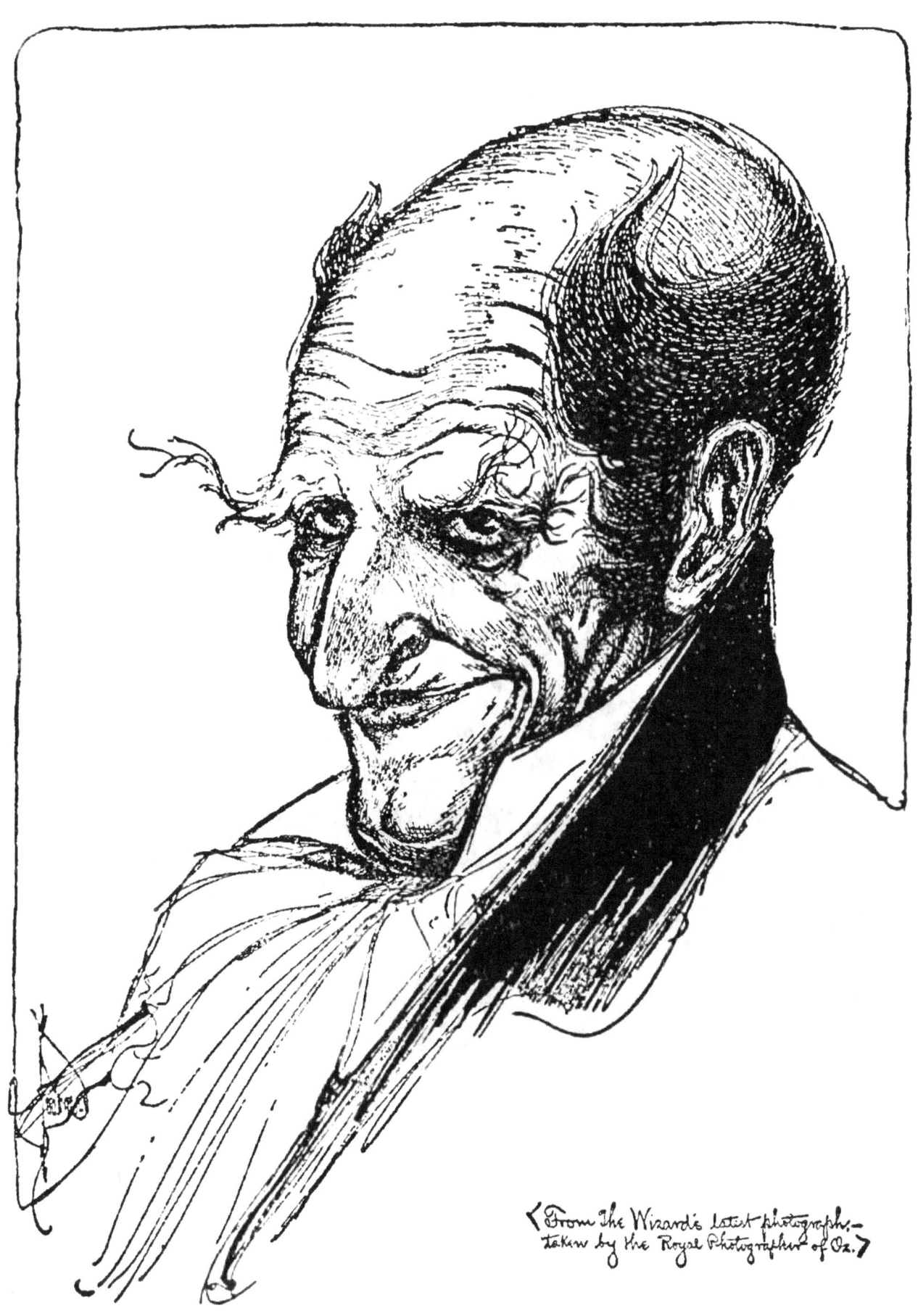

From the Wizard's latest photograph taken by the Royal Photographer of Oz.

PORTRAIT OF THE WIZARD OF OZ

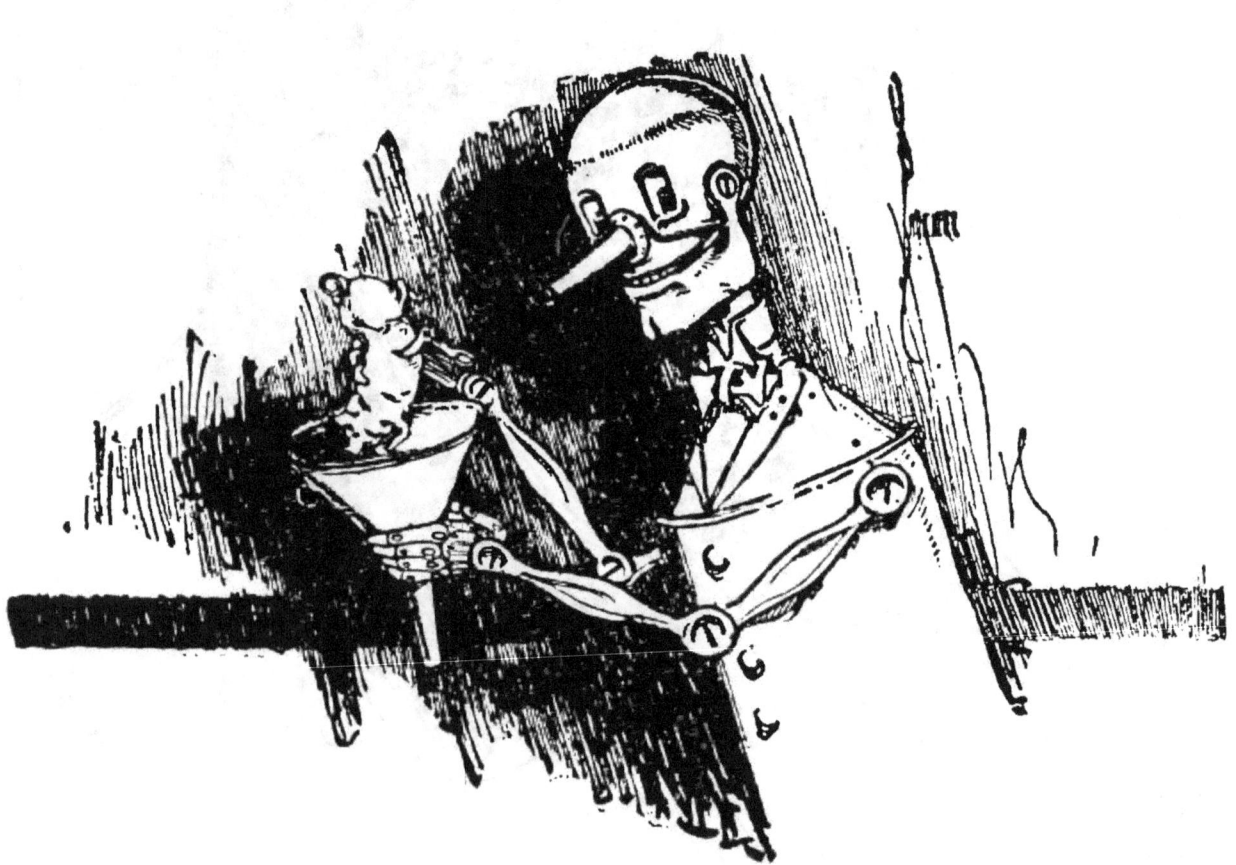

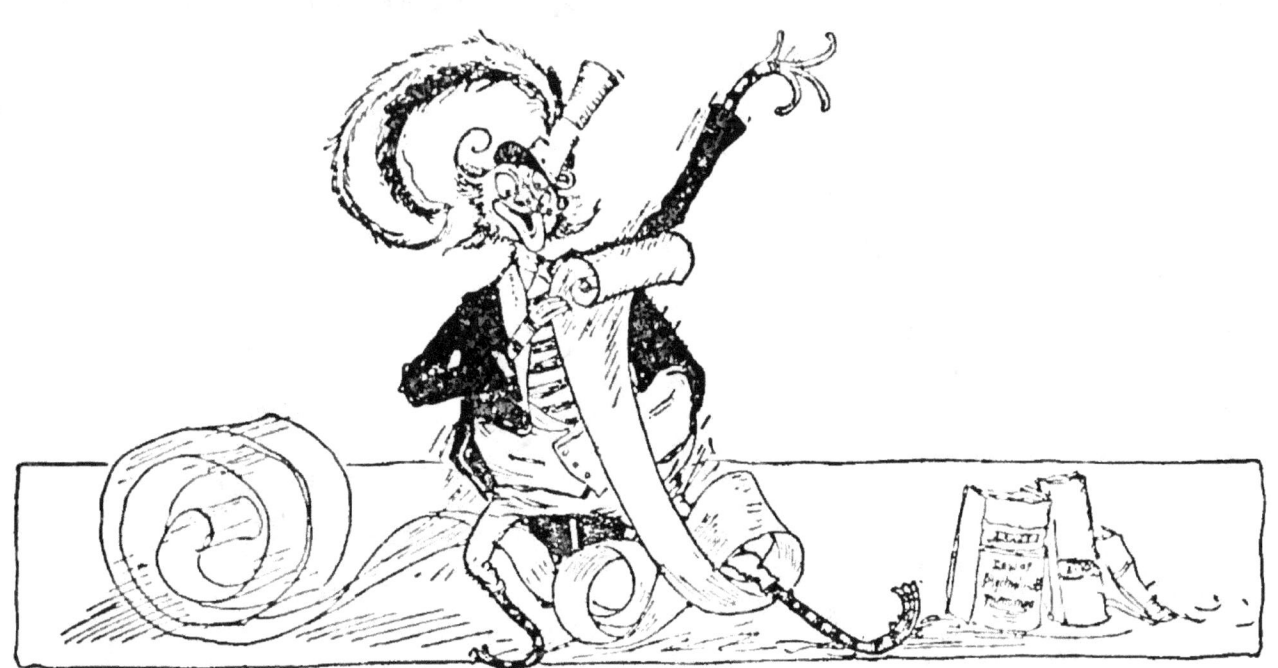

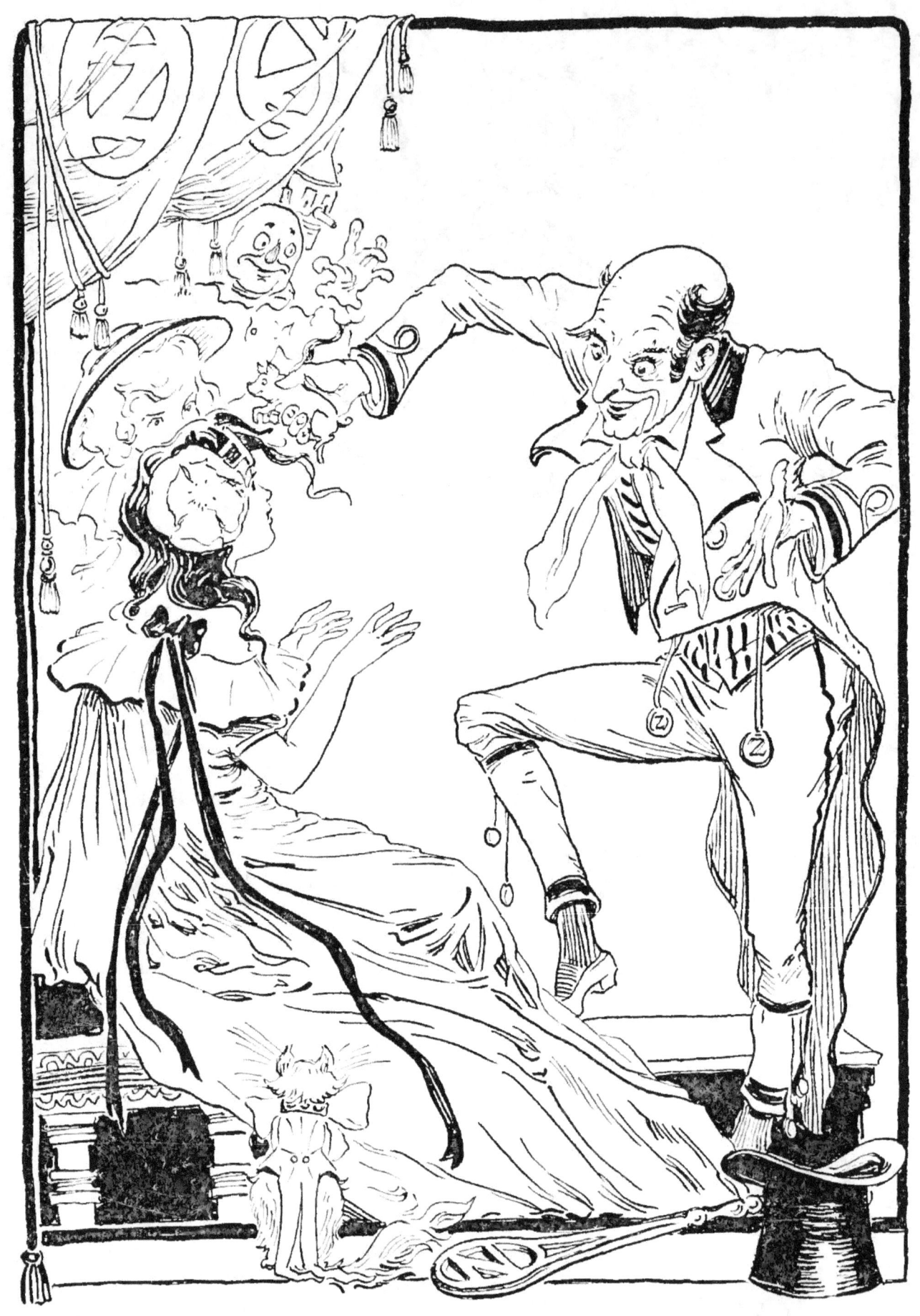

THE WIZARD PERFORMS ANOTHER TRICK

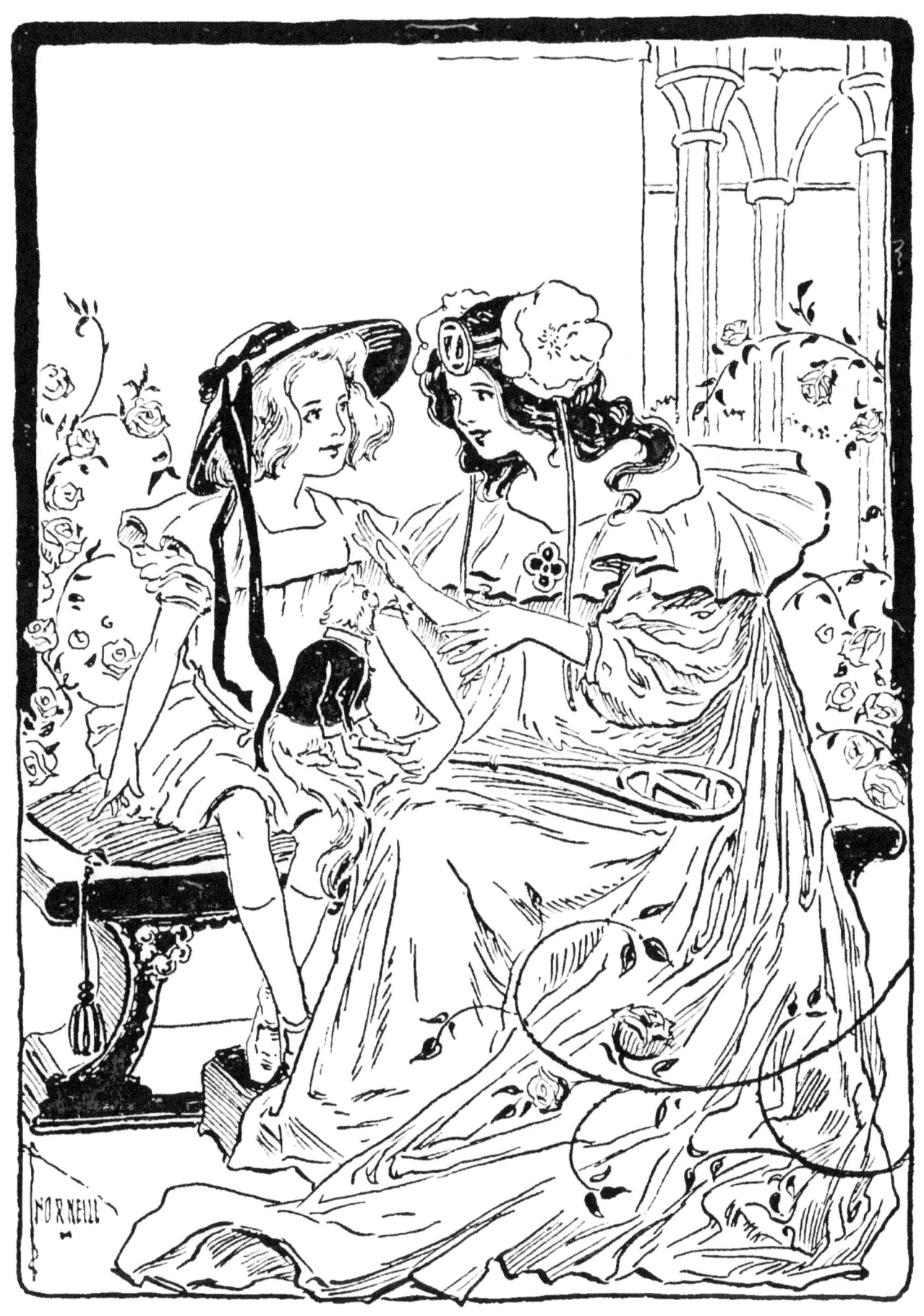

DOROTHY AND OZMA

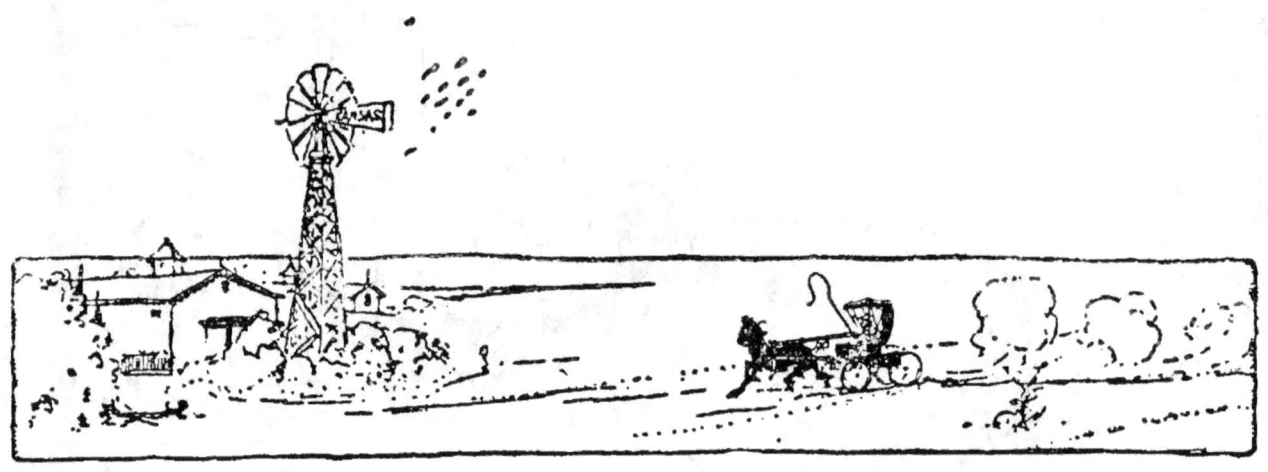

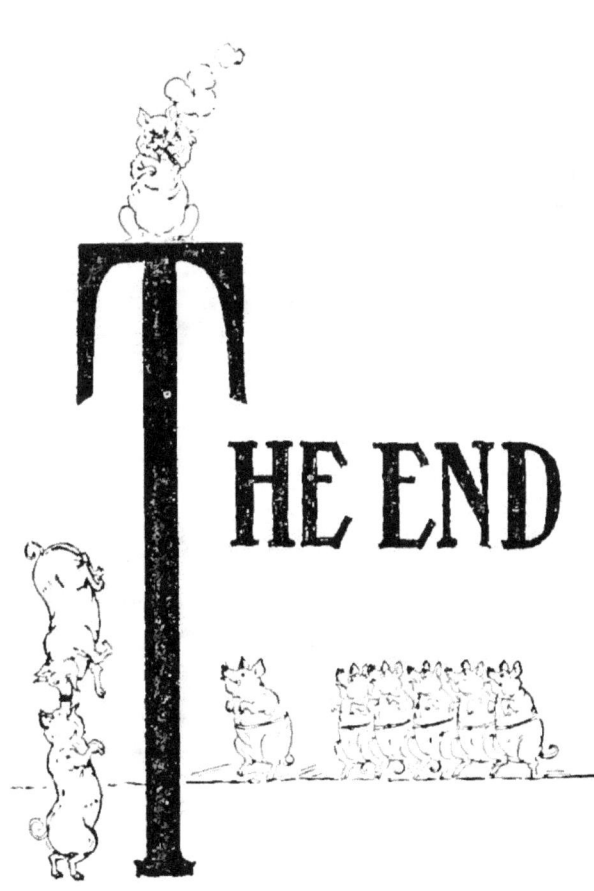

THE END